The Great Country Houses
of Poland

The Great

COUNTRY HOUSES
OF
POLAND

Michael Pratt
Photography by Gerhard Trumler

Abbeville Press Publishers
New York · London

In fond memory of Josef and Gina Liechtenstein, who inspired me to write this book, and Ian Moncreiffe, whose esoteric historical scholarship I have sorely missed.

Editor: Constance Herndon
Designer: Molly Shields
Jacket Designers: Ada Blazer and Misha Beletsky
Production Editors: Lanie Davis and Erin Dress
Production Supervisors: Hope Koturo and Louise Kurtz
Map Illustrator: Sophie Kittredge

Library of Congress Cataloging-in-Publication Data

Pratt, Michael, Lord.
  The great country houses of Poland / by Lord Michael Pratt ; photographs by Gerhard Trumler. — 1st ed.
      p. cm.
  Includes bibliographical references and index.
  ISBN-13: 978-0-7892-0890-3 (alk. paper)
  1. Castles—Poland. 2. Manors—Poland. I. Title.

  NA7763.P73 2007
  728.809438—dc22
                            2006030591

Printed and bound in China.

First edition

10 9 8 7 6 5 4 3 2 1

Front cover: Corner view of main facade at Baranów.
Back cover: Billiard room, Kozłówka.
Page 1: Ceiling in the Tower Room, Baranów.
Frontispiece: Interior of Izabela Lubomirska's bathroom, Wilanów.
Page 5: Grotesque head with foliage painted by Szymon Mankowski, Nieborów.

Note: Unless otherwise indicated in the caption, all objects and pictures illustrated are from the collections of the houses featured in the chapter.

For bulk, and premium sales and for text adoption procedures, write to Customer Service Manager, Abbeville Press, 137 Varick Street, New York, NY 10013, or call 1-800-ARTBOOK.

Visit Abbeville Press online at www.abbeville.com.

CONTENTS

ACKNOWLEDGMENTS

For help with the publication and rewriting of this book, I am indebted to:

Within Poland: Princess Mary Sapieha; Prince Christoph Radziwill; Count & Countess Jan Tarnowski; Count Stanislaus Czartoryski; Count Marek Potocki; Count Andrew Zoltowski; Count Marcin Zamoyski and the Staff of the Tourist office, Zamosc; Mme. Anna Wolska; Dr. & Mrs. Milewska; Mme. Marie Osterba (Krakow); Dr. Franciszek Cemka (Ministry of Culture); Professor Rottermund and the Staff of the Royal Castle, Warsaw; The Staff of the Wawel Museum, Krakow

The Directors and Staff at: Wilanow; Łazienki; Nieborow; Puławy; Kozłowka; Łańcut; Pieskowa Skała

And last, but not least, Roman, who drove us perfectly round Poland.

In London: Count Adam Zamoyski; Mlle. Elzbieta Łubienska; Mr. & Mrs. Jan Pomian; Mr. & Mrs. Alexander Schneider; H.E. Dr. Cezary Kroll, Acting Polish Ambassador, and staff

My loyal wife Janet, who accompanied me throughout this trip

Fiona Campbell, for legal advice

Jane Manley, for deciphering and organising my MSS

Abbeville Press of New York City for a chance to publish this book

M. P.
May 2007

PREFACE

Sixteen years have elapsed since the publication of *The Great Country Houses of Central Europe*. During that time, enormous changes have occurred. Following the downfall of Communism, Poland has now joined both NATO and the EU. Although the capitalist and democratic identities of Polish society is not yet fully established and the formerly Communist politicians are still sometimes returned to power by the ballot box, Poland is nevertheless making huge strides in the right direction.

Poland has paradoxically proved the slowest and most disappointing of all the four Central European countries featured in the original volume to effect a genuine process of restitution. Only in Poland had the aristocracy ever remained in any number. Almost all those aristocrats hardy enough to have stayed on under a Communist government initially left Hungary and the Czech Republic: in Hungary en masse after the crushing of the 1956 uprising, and in the Czech lands after the Prague Spring of 1969 had been suppressed. In Poland many aristocrats kept a low profile and yet managed to survive as respected members of their local communities, sometimes even retaining some ties to their former properties. It appeared that a more cohesive society had been somehow kept alive, despite all their rulers' attempts to clone everyone as Marxist man.

Sadly, legitimate restitution has not taken place, and empirical rather than ethical considerations have taken on the greatest importance. To return to the pre-1939 landholdings has simply proved too controversial for any government to wish to tackle. In contrast to the other eastern European countries, in Poland state co-operatives had been the norm, and the agricultural land had been divided between umpteen tiny peasant proprietors, each fiercely attached to his own small holding. The Warsaw government has often seemed ready to give back houses in urgent need of repair, provided they are of no public interest and scant historical importance.

All Polish houses that rank as integral part of their country's heritage have stayed in the hands of the state. It is deemed right to allow the public interest to override private ones, thus major properties such as Nieborow or Wilanów have not been returned, in defiance of legitimate family claims. The state has pursued a cynical policy of encouraging émigrés to return with their money from America or Western Europe, provided there is no conflict with the state's interest. Naturally no former German estates in Silesia, Pomerania or Polish East Prussia have been offered back, while properties such as the Radziwills at Niełwieł and Ołyka, no longer within the nation's modern frontiers, remain almost as remote as ever.

Despite the terrible destruction wrought upon the country house heritage of Central Europe during the past sixty-five years, however, there is hope for more restitution and preservation in the coming years.

M. P.
2007

In preparing this new Preface, particular thanks are due to: Baroness Elmar von Haxthausen, Count Adam Zamoyski, Prince Friedrich zu Schwarzenberg, Prince George Festetics, Christopher Hudson, and Jane Manley.

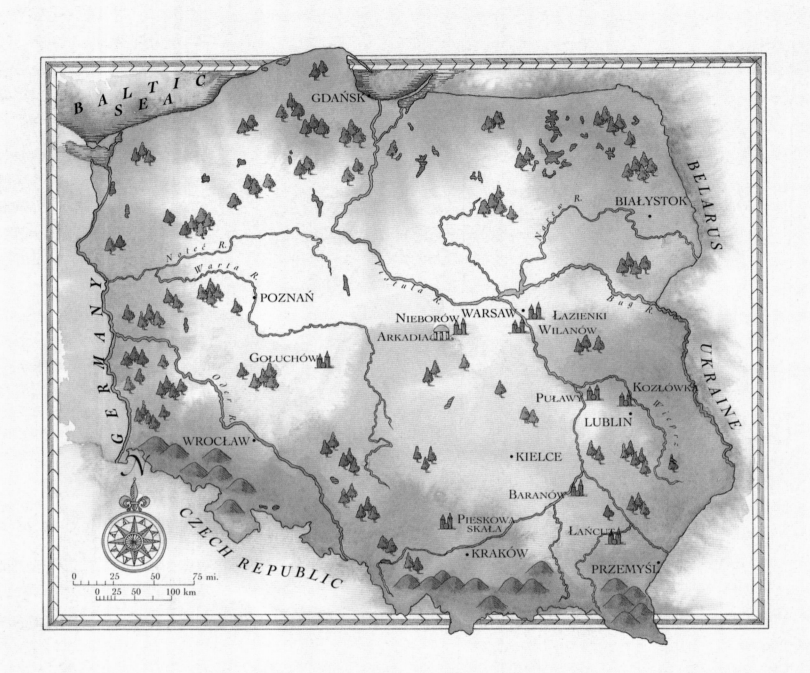

etween the Hammer and the Anvil is the title of a fairly recent history of Poland, an aptly chosen one indeed, for the country has been ground between the German hammer and the Russian anvil for the past millennium. The Poles at one time ruled the largest state in Europe, but their nation lacked natural frontiers; later on it was erased from the map for over a century. Theirs has been a past both heroic and tragic.

Both of these traits were exemplified by the *szlachta*, as the gentry and the nobility were called. For centuries they constituted the political nation in Poland, a phenomenon unique in Europe, and were largely responsible both for their country's rise to greatness and for its decline into partition and foreign occupation. Thanks to the repeated devastation that Poland has undergone, the houses and castles of the *szlachta* are in quite variable condition and some no longer even stand on Polish soil, yet they provide an eloquent memorial to a remarkable class.

If an arbitrary starting date is necessary, Poland's history can be said to have begun in the mid-tenth century. Before that the country existed in relative isolation, for a ring of Slavic tribes shut it off from the outside world—indeed the Roman Empire had never penetrated anywhere near its boundaries. The Poles were an agrarian people living in self-sufficient village communities, yet sharing a common language, religion, and way of life. By the tenth century, however, the Piast dynasty had established its rule over a relatively wide area and had developed a fiscal system and a small standing army. When the Holy Roman emperor Otto I encountered it on his eastern campaign in 955, Poland's ruler, Prince Mieszko I, realized that isolation was no longer possible. Aware of the benefits that his neighbors the Bohemians had derived from Christianity—principally that it would remove the emperor's pretext of conversion for subjugating his people—he decided that his people, too, should be converted. After his own baptism and with Otto's approval he married a Christian Bohemian princess, and in 966 the Duchy of Polonia became a part of Christendom. Nevertheless Mieszko continued his independent policies most successfully, fighting the Germans again several times, adding Silesia and Pomerania to his dominions (and thereby control of the Baltic seaboard), and repulsing a Russian invasion by Vladimir the Great. At about that time Russia was converted by missionaries from the Eastern Orthodox Church, and its consequent alignment with Byzantium, in contrast to Poland's with Rome, foreshadowed a good number of future conflicts between the two nations.

Mieszko's son Bolesław the Brave succeeded in 992. A brilliant soldier and politician, he persuaded the pope to make Gniezno into an archepiscopal see and create three other Polish bishoprics, thus underlining the Polish Church's independence. The Empire was alternately friendly and hostile, but Bolesław contained the military threat and had himself crowned king of Poland in 1025, shortly before his death. Unfortunately his achievement did not endure. The two weak rulers who followed and the regional factionalism that resulted from the country's rapid enlargement led to a period of decline. One king lost his throne by quarrelling with the papacy and his successor was forced by the nobility to carve up his kingdom into five duchies of equal status for his five sons. But a national consciousness had begun to evolve, and the country's economy had started to develop. By 1100 over eighty castle towns existed, while cities like Kraków, the capital, Sandomierz, Wrocław, and Poznań, were solidly established. Nevertheless, rival claims between the larger towns and the regional lords meant that Poland continued to fragment, for having evolved from clanlike structures, its society was not feudal in the western sense.

At the bottom of twelfth-century Poland's economic and social hierarchy stood the peasantry, still mostly free and not tied to the land. During the next century, however, an agrarian boom meant that peasants who

Map of modern Poland showing locations of major country houses.

owned land thrived, but the landless peasants, who had nothing but their labor to offer, increasingly became tied to the land in a form of economic vassalage. At the top of the social scale the gentry or *szlachta* inherited both their status and the lands over which they acted as independent magistrates, although they were obliged to perform military service for their ruler and submit to his courts.

The nascent middle class was represented by the settlers in the towns, who were largely foreigners. The towns had evolved as separate entities, distinct from the surrounding countryside thanks to their royal charters and governed by German rather than Polish customary law. These developments tended to weaken royal power, still exercised by directly appointed officials called castellans. However these officials were increasingly superseded by the *voyevods* or palatines, who administered the various duchies.

The Mongol invasion of 1241 devastated Poland and further exacerbated the difficulty of achieving national unity. Fortunately it was of short duration, but the Mongols returned twice more in the course of the century, depopulating the south and east. The vulnerability of the divided country was exposed, just as it was by the growing power of the Teutonic Knights, whom Duke Konrad of Mazovia had foolishly invited in 1226 to subdue the heathen Prussians. The Order's ruthless warfare and skillful diplomacy enabled them to conquer all of Prussia and Polish Pomerania by 1300. Together with the newly emergent Margravate of Brandenburg to the west, they threatened Polish access to the Baltic. Meanwhile German settlers were pouring into the country to replace the population lost by the Mongol invasions, and the resulting anti-Teutonic feelings fueled the drive for reunification. Duke Władysław the Short of Kraków forged an alliance with Angevin Hungary, and with papal approval embarked on the

Szlachta *from various regions of Poland in national dress, late sixteenth century.* (Łańcut *collection.*)

reconquest of the country, but it was his son Kazimierz the Great who completed the task. During the latter fourteenth century, even as Western Europe was ravaged by the Hundred Years' War and the Black Death, the Poles enjoyed an era of relative peace and prosperity.

With the spread of Christianity throughout the country, the Romanesque style pervaded Poland with churches built mostly in stone. The first traces of Polish Romanesque were timid enough, small rotundas erected near the major castles in the late tenth century, but within a hundred years, towered two-aisled basilicas were being constructed, already showing Rhenish influence. By the twelfth century religious artifacts of a high standard were being produced, and monasteries were being established. Along with the cathedral schools, the latter became the main educational force in the land, even if their pious zeal was notably lacking. In the realm of secular as opposed to ecclesiastical architecture, the short supply of good quality building stone meant that residences were almost entirely wooden, sometimes reinforced by clay and stone—although Bolesław the Brave appears to have had a stone palace as early as 1000. Fortresses multiplied both as administrative centers and to satisfy military needs in the endless feuds between the Piast duchies.

In Wielkopolska or Greater Poland (the western region around Gniezno and Poznań) much Romanesque building took place, more commonly in stone than in Malopolska or Lesser Poland (the southern area around Kraków). In the early thirteenth century, however, the introduction of brick enormously stimulated construction, especially in the triangle formed by Kraków, Kielce, and Sandomierz, the core of the late-medieval Polish kingdom. Further north in Pomerania and along the Baltic coast, brick was used almost exclusively for both churches and castles, stone being employed only for door and window casings and for decorative details. The Gothic style had already arrived before 1300, thanks mainly to the Cistercians, but was properly established by the ambitious building program of Kazimierz the Great. Gniezno and Kraków cathedrals, along with a mass of other churches and castles constructed during these years, were fitting monuments to his reign, which also saw the fortification of old towns and the foundation of new. In these urban areas the architecture reflected the inhabitants' growing opulence and elegance. On the Wawel Hill in Kraków the king created his own stronghold by replacing the upper castle and its adjoining rampart protected by a moat and earthworks with walls of dressed stone and a central gate. Laid out around a large courtyard, the Gothic design remained until the great fire of 1499 and the subsequent alterations.

Kazimierz was indeed aptly named "the Great." In 1333 he had succeeded to a weak, poor, and backward realm only recently reunited by his father. He proceeded to overhaul the fiscal and monetary systems, create a central chancellery, codify the whole corpus of existing laws, and establish guilds in the towns. Favorable climatic conditions encouraged an agrarian boom, and industry—especially mining, which uncovered new deposits—expanded dramatically. An influx of refugees from Western Europe brought in artisans and merchants while the Church's promotion of studies abroad meant that Polish scholars and poets became known throughout the continent. In 1364 Kraków University was founded, the second of its kind in Central Europe after that in Prague.

A good central government and fair justice were complemented by skillful diplomacy, on which the king relied more than on warfare. He never surrendered his claims to Silesia and Pomerania, lost earlier to Bohemia and the Teutonic Knights respectively, but he did reincorporate Mazovia (the region round Płock and Warsaw) into his dominions, which he almost redoubled by conquering Podolia and Volhynia to the southeast. Here the population was Orthodox rather than Roman Catholic and Ruthene rather than ethnic Polish. Yet even as Kazimierz supported the spread of Catholicism, he allowed wide religious freedom. The Polish Commonwealth, which was to stretch from the Baltic to the Black Sea, had been inaugurated. Fittingly toward the end of his reign the king played host to a glittering summit of his fellow monarchs discussing the possibility of a new crusade.

On his death in 1370, Kazimierz left no legitimate male heir, instead bequeathing his throne to his nephew Louis of Hungary. When he too died twelve years later, the "Kraków lords," who effectively ran the country, chose Louis's ten-year-old younger daughter, Jadwiga, for their queen. Disregarding the child's protests that she was already betrothed to William of Habsburg, they married her off to the pagan grand duke of Lithuania, twenty-six years her senior. After Władysław (as he had been renamed) had been baptized, the couple married in the Wawel's cathedral in 1386 and simultaneously the two kingdoms merged. Poland's destiny for the next four centuries was to be linked to Lithuania, its backward eastern neighbor and three times its size. The union may have been of dubious benefit in the long term, but in the short run it bolstered national security and brought in a vigorous new dynasty, the Jagellon, to rule the country. Also of significance was the fact that the nobility had willingly chosen a foreign king, a development that in effect ensured a constitutional monarchy in the future.

Although Jadwiga's marriage was childless and she died young, Władysław reigned on until 1434. A joint Polish-Lithuanian army routed the Teutonic Knights at Grunwald in 1410 and they were defeated again several times during the next decades. Nevertheless the Polish king avoided crushing the order, for it had powerful friends in the papacy and the Empire whom he hesitated to alienate. Besides, his government, which advocated religious tolerance, was branded schismatic at the Council of Constance in 1415 and he had no wish to have a crusade launched against him. Moreover the union of Lithuania, a nation of pagan Balts and Orthodox Slavs, with the far more developed Poland remained uneasy. Nevertheless by 1500, after the Jagellon rulers had gained the thrones of Bohemia and Hungary as well, the dynasty ruled over a third of the European mainland. After the young King Ludwik fell fighting the Turks at Mohács in 1526, both realms passed to the Habsburgs.

Under the Jagellons and free from foreign invasions, Poland enjoyed its golden age. Its political institutions assumed a definite shape and the principle of government by consensus between the crown and the seyms or assemblies was now firmly established. Each province had its own seym composed of representatives of the *szlachta*, although the crown did not summon them too frequently. The castellans and palatines were granted seats on the Grand Council during the fifteenth century but it was the Privy Council, dominated by a caucus of palatines and bishops, that wielded the real power and dictated the succession. Not surprisingly the *szlachta* objected to the concentration of power in the hands of this oligarchy, so when Kazimierz IV sought their support in the 1450s they demanded in return that no troops or taxes could be raised by the crown without the consent of the eighteen provincial seyms. Thus the principle of no taxation without representation ensured the *szlachta* a voice. The National Seym, which by the sixteenth century represented Mazovia as well as Wielkopolska and Małopolska, was now split between the Senate, containing the bishops and administrative office holders, and the Lower Chamber, consisting of deputies from the *szlachta* and the larger cities.

By the sixteenth century the crown's power was so circumscribed that it could not be used arbitrarily. The Seym closely vetted each new king before electing him, even if he was the only son of his predecessor. The new county courts, with their centrally appointed sheriffs or starostas and judges, were constantly challenged by the seyms, by the manorial courts, and above all by the ecclesiastical tribunals, all of which had overlapping areas of jurisdiction. Legislative functions were taken over by the Seym, which spoke for the enfranchised ten percent of the population and could plausibly claim to be more representative than any other comparable contemporary body.

The system, however, had an inherent weakness, for it had developed exclusively in the interests of one class, which was restricted both in its vision and composition. The *szlachta's* privileged status was enshrined by the neminem captivabimus statute, a forerunner of habeas corpus that guaranteed their freedom from arrest or punishment except under due process of law, and by the nihil novi statute, which required that the crown take no action without endorsement by both chambers of the Seym. With their bitter internecine rivalries and fierce class solidarity, the *szlachta* had little in common with the feudal nobilities of Western Europe. Even their coats of arms were never personal to the bearer and were borne by all members of a family impartially, often by families of different names that may have shared a common origin. Perhaps their closest parallel was to the Scottish clan system. Father Stanisław Orzechowski remarked on the *szlachta's* remarkable status in the mid-sixteenth century. "Consider the Pole's position in the world"—and by Poles he meant the *szlachta*—"proud in his freedom, resplendent in his liberties, dressed in the glorious robe of rights equal with those of the King. That is why the

Distant view of Pieskowa Skała, near Kraków.

Nobles in Polish costume, early seventeenth century.
(Gołuchów collection.)

Pole wears the fine gold ring of nobility, which makes equals of the highest and the lowest in the land."

By the sixteenth century Poland had become the granary of Europe, and during this period the *szlachta* grew rich. The labor days tenants worked in lieu of rent were increased from twelve to fifty-two per annum, thereby imposing a form of economic serfdom since most could not afford to move away. Hitherto estates had remained small by Western European standards but now the magnates in particular became large landowners—the Tarnowski family, for example, doubled the size of their properties. Taken by itself the yield from land could still not produce a high enough income for the ambitions of many members of this class, so lucrative public office and business ventures, especially mining, became necessary supplements. Thus many families like the Szafraniec based themselves near the larger cities where some of their newfound wealth was soon to be channeled into artistic patronage.

The growth of prosperity in fifteenth-century Poland combined with the increase in the local population and in immigration from the West fostered much building activity. In the north the Teutonic Knights brought in Flemish architects, whose massive city walls and ecclesiastical and civic buildings can still be seen; in central Poland, on the other hand, in Mazovia and Wielkopolska, a modified local style predominated that harked back to a lighter German-Burgundian Gothic most akin to Bohemian architecture. Churches like Saint Mary's in Kraków were continually modified: the wonderful stellar vaulting there and the charming steeples were later additions. Ornamentation was normally plain in comparison with the rich work found in France or Flanders, but in eastern Poland a surprising result of the union with Lithuania was the fine frescoes of Russo-Byzantine provenance executed in some churches such as the chapel at Lublin Castle.

Secular architecture now began to assume the same importance as ecclesiastical. Innumerable fine town halls and burghers' houses were built reconquest of the country, but it was his son Kazimierz the Great who completed the task. During the latter fourteenth century, even as Western Europe was ravaged by the Hundred Years' War and the Black Death, the Poles enjoyed an era of relative peace and prosperity.

With the spread of Christianity throughout the country, the Romanesque style pervaded Poland with churches built mostly in stone. The first traces of Polish Romanesque were timid enough, small rotundas erected near the major castles in the late tenth century, but within a hundred years, towered two-aisled basilicas were being constructed, already showing Rhenish influence. By the twelfth century religious artifacts of a high standard were being produced, and monasteries were being established. Along with the cathedral schools, the latter became the main educational force in the land, even if their pious zeal was notably lacking. In the realm of secular as opposed to ecclesiastical architecture, the short supply of good quality building stone meant that residences were almost entirely wooden, sometimes reinforced by clay and stone—although Bolesław the Brave appears to have had a stone palace as early as 1000. Fortresses multiplied both as administrative centers and to satisfy military needs in the endless feuds between the Piast duchies.

In Wielkopolska or Greater Poland (the western region around Gniezno and Poznań) much Romanesque building took place, more commonly in stone than in Malopolska or Lesser Poland (the southern area around Kraków). In the early thirteenth century, however, the introduction of brick enormously stimulated construction, especially in the triangle formed by Kraków, Kielce, and Sandomierz, the core of the late-medieval Polish kingdom. Further north in Pomerania and along the Baltic coast, brick was used almost exclusively for both churches and castles, stone being employed only for door and window casings and for decorative details. The Gothic style had already arrived before 1300, thanks mainly to the Cistercians, but was properly established by the ambitious building program of Kazimierz the Great. Gniezno and Kraków cathedrals, along with a mass of other churches and castles constructed during these years, were fitting monuments to his reign, which also saw the fortification of old towns and the foundation of new. In these urban areas the architecture reflected the inhabitants' growing opulence and elegance. On the Wawel Hill in Kraków the king created his own stronghold by replacing the upper castle and its adjoining rampart protected by a moat and earthworks with walls of dressed stone and a central gate. Laid out around a large courtyard, the Gothic design remained until the great fire of 1499 and the subsequent alterations.

Kazimierz was indeed aptly named "the Great." In 1333 he had succeeded to a weak, poor, and backward realm only recently reunited by his father. He proceeded to overhaul the fiscal and monetary systems, create a central chancellery, codify the whole corpus of existing laws, and establish guilds in the towns. Favorable climatic conditions encouraged an agrarian boom, and industry—especially mining, which uncovered new deposits—expanded dramatically. An influx of refugees from Western Europe brought in artisans and merchants while the Church's promotion of studies abroad meant that Polish scholars and poets became known throughout the continent. In 1364 Kraków University was founded, the second of its kind in Central Europe after that in Prague.

A good central government and fair justice were complemented by skillful diplomacy, on which the king relied more than on warfare. He never surrendered his claims to Silesia and Pomerania, lost earlier to Bohemia and the Teutonic Knights respectively, but he did reincorporate Mazovia (the region round Płock and Warsaw) into his dominions, which he almost redoubled by conquering Podolia and Volhynia to the southeast. Here the population was Orthodox rather than Roman Catholic and Ruthene rather than ethnic Polish. Yet even as Kazimierz supported the west, gaining many converts among the German populations of the towns and few elsewhere. In an astonishing about-face, Grand Master Albrecht von Hohenzollern converted to Lutheranism and secularized the Teutonic Order in 1625, being granted the duchy of Prussia by a formal act of homage to Zygmunt I. The arrival of Calvinism was more significant; with its democratic organization and its eschewal of pomp and ceremony it swept the country, appealing especially to the *szlachta*, who were traditionally suspicious of the power of the Catholic Church. Extremer sects were also tolerated, including Anabaptists, Mennonites, and even the Arians, who rejected the Trinity and the divinity of Christ. By the 1550s a majority of deputies to the Seym were Protestants, as were members of the Senate by the 1570s. Many magnate families like the Leszczyńskis and Radziwiłłs had converted to Calvinism, and even some prelates remained open-minded: Andrzej Zebrzydowski, bishop of Kraków, told his congregation they could worship a goat if they went on paying their tithes. King Zygmunt I made it clear that the religious debate was none of his business, while many of the most staunchly Catholic among the *szlachta* sided with the Calvinists if they felt that liberty was imperiled by persecutions. In 1555 a majority of the delegates to the Seym demanded the establishment of a Polish church independent of Rome.

The indecisive Zygmunt August faced a dilemma: to do nothing was obviously impossible, but he feared to do too much. Therefore he referred the Seym's demands to Rome, where the pope promptly condemned them as heretical and left it at that. The Protestants, divided by internal squabbles and lacking a strong leader, had missed their chance. Yet the Reformation in Poland was really less of a spiritual movement than a vehicle for the intellectual and political emancipation of the upper classes, embodied in the executionist movement, which demanded an end to the Catholic Church's immunity from taxation and the diocesan courts. Slowly the Counter-Reformation gained momentum. Its tactics were moderate for its spokesman, Cardinal Hosius, was an articulate and decent man. It was he who introduced the Jesuits to Poland, and one of their luminaries, Piotr Skarga, wielded enormous influence as confessor to the king and chaplain to the Seym. Gradually reconversions occurred; Mikołaj Radziwiłł abjured his father's Protestantism, setting a pattern for many of his peers. Persecutions were substantially avoided and where mixed marriages still occurred they worked eventually to the Catholics' advantage, since the children were brought up in the Church. Freedom of religion was enshrined in the constitution in 1573 with the Confederation of Warsaw and remained an element of Polish policy even after the majority of Protestants had peacefully returned to the Roman fold.

The Reformation was not the only problem worrying the Poles in the late sixteenth century, however—the end to the dynasty was also in sight. King Zygmunt August was a sad figure, the only son of Zygmunt I and the sinister Milanese, Bona Sforza. His first wife, Elizabeth of Habsburg, had died after two years of marriage, while his great love, the beautiful Barbara Radziwiłł, also perished four years after their elopement; both were reputedly poisoned by his mother. He refused to touch his third wife, the epileptic Katherine of Habsburg, and so remained childless. Some of the *szlachta* were concerned. With the Union of Lublin in 1569, the Polish and Lithuanian Seyms had merged. Although they retained separate laws, treasuries, and armies, they formally shared one monarch and one combined Seym, which met in the small Mazovian city of Warsaw, the future capital. The dearest wish of most of the *szlachta* for a "royal republic," which was what the Most Serene Commonwealth of the two nations of Poland and Lithuania actually was, had been granted. But there was no question of managing without a king. Unfortunately nothing had been agreed about the succession by the time Zygmunt August died in 1572.

During the sixteenth century the development of Polish architecture

Detail of fortifications at Pieskowa Skała.

had been spectacular and had led to the creation of some of the finest Renaissance monuments in Europe. The Renaissance style had reached Poland in two ways. From Hungary—where it had been in evidence since 1450 and with which there was a dynastic link—the Renaissance arrived via highly accomplished Tuscan craftsmen who brought Italian sculpture and architecture to Kraków; from there it spread to other areas of the Jagellonian realm. From centers in Western Europe the new trends gradually infiltrated the Gothic tradition in every field of the arts, and the two currents merged at Kraków.

On his accession in 1506, Zygmunt I had determined to rebuild Kraków's fire-damaged Wawel, and he commissioned the recently established Italian atelier of his protégé Francis the Florentine for this purpose. Work began immediately on the Queen's House, as the Wawel's west facade was known, and for three decades a steady stream of prepared lime- and sandstone was sent up the hill. The splendid inner courtyard, three stories high with arcades around the two lower levels, conformed to the precepts laid down by Vitruvius—although by Polish custom the state apartments were located on the top floor, not on the _piano nobile_ as in Italy. The steeply pitched roof, another local refinement, was supported by a series of columns rising through the whole of the upper story, their height tempered only by the rings binding the shafts, while their capitals directly supported the eaves.

Francis died in 1516, to be succeeded by his compatriot Bartolomeo Berrecci, likewise a sculptor as well as an architect. From 1517 to 1533 Berrecci with his entire atelier labored on the burial chapel for King Zygmunt, located near the courtyard and resting against the south aisle of the Wawel's cathedral. The result, with its fairly plain exterior and its sumptuously decorated interior, is a sophisticated Renaissance building, perhaps the finest Italian exemplar of its date north of the Alps. The Berrecci

17

atelier also executed other commissions such as the oratory and pres-
bytery of Saint Mary's Church in Kraków, which housed a superb late-
Gothic carved altarpiece by Wit Stwosz, and two grandiose tombs, of
Bishop Piotr Tomicki at the Wawel, and of Barbara Tarnowska at Tarnów
Cathedral.

As well as Italian architects, Polish, Slovak, and German craftsmen
were involved in pioneering a transitional style from the Gothic to the
Renaissance. In these early years the work of this local school, which was
responsible for buildings like the castle at Drzewica, was more widespread
than that of the Italians. Their main representative was a royal architect
simply known as Benedykt of Sandomierz, who was given the responsibil-
ity for designing several dozen portals and window frames in the Wawel
since there were not enough Italian craftsmen to do everything. Here
late-Gothic patterns mingle with Renaissance ornament without any attempt at integration. Other elements in the Wawel's decoration also combined both styles.

At Berrecci's death in 1537, his place was taken by Giovanni Maria
Padovano. But rival ateliers had now sprung up such as that founded a few
years earlier by Bernardino de Gianotis and Giovanni Cini. These two architects built the new cathedral at Płock for Bishop Tomicki's nephew and
the castle of Ogrodzieniec in Małopolska for the banking dynasty of
Boner. The latter is a good example of the Renaissance fortress as was
Ostróg in Volhynia, seat of the Princes Ostrogski, where huge buttresses
reached down to the river. By the 1520s other Italian craftsmen from
Ticino and Como had arrived too. Of more modest aspirations, they represented a less purely Italianate style, unattached to the Gothic but more
sensitive to local traditions.

By the mid-sixteenth century the Renaissance style in Poland had assumed an independent standing—at least in architecture and sculpture,
for painting played a far less important role. (Indeed no Italian painter is
known to have visited the country before 1540.) The geographical spread

Domed tower at Krasiczyn with Renaissance
sgraffiti, southeastern Poland.

of the style was ensured since it was widely disseminated throughout the urban patricians and the more prosperous of the *szlachta*, who were building country houses of their own. For in the towns Renaissance architecture had blossomed as town halls and Gothic mansions were modernized or reconstructed; in Tarnów or Sandomierz, relatively small stylistically pure civic buildings were produced with simple, nearly cubic forms and facades closed horizontally by the attic parapets. Best of them all was the Poznań Town Hall (entirely rebuilt between 1550 and 1560 by Giovanni Battista Quadro), which was plastered with sgraffiti. Its loggia and staircase were similar to those that embellished the Cloth Hall in Kraków reconstructed by Padovano during the 1550s.

The Italian high and late Renaissance still decided the general character of the period's architecture. Treatises like Sebastiano Serlio's were influential, as were copies of the northern European mannerist engravings. Kraków remained the artistic center, full of ateliers engaged in decorative and figurative sculpture as well as in architecture. A few Dutch and German craftsmen arrived but most of the new practitioners were Polish. The Italians formed a closed circle no longer, blending ever more closely with their adopted country.

Despite the general supremacy of Italian Renaissance traditions, the style did not completely dominate developments in Poland. Penetrating Pomerania spasmodically, it secured only a tiny foothold in Gdańsk, where the Gothic continued to flourish. The emergence of local schools of architecture meant furthermore that Kraków's ability to create a uniform style diminished—in western and eastern Poland, for instance, numerous craftsmen propagated a decorative vernacular northern Italian version of the Renaissance. Continuity was also hampered by the fact that most buildings were not new but had been converted from the Gothic.

A distinctive feature of the national style first used in urban architecture was the Polish "attic." Designed as a decorative parapet wall to mask the roof, it was given specific constructional and functional tasks and became very imposing and ornate. Normally running around the entire building, it isolated terrace roofs from one another and prevented the spread of fire. The visible parts were richly decorated with ornament varying from late Gothic crenellations to Venetian pinnacled crests. Often attics were extended upward and given a lower tier divided by pilasters, columns, or blind arcading, and a crowning ridge indented with spheres, volutes, pinnacles, or socles. Almost their first recorded appearance was in midcentury, on Kraków's Cloth Hall, but the fashion quickly spread throughout the country.

The other characteristic feature that developed in Polish architecture during this period was the arcaded loggia. Although the Wawel provided the celebrated original example, the element became commonly used in country houses, the number of which, whether new projects or conversions, markedly increased in the second half of the sixteenth century. Of the new projects the royal hunting lodge built by the Polish architect Tomasz Grzymała for Zygmunt August at Niepołomice (1550–71) was a landmark of purely residential rather than defensive design. The best of the conversions included the enlargements of the castles at Wilno and Tęczyn. An outstanding new Florentine architect named Santi Gucci arrived in Kraków during the 1550s and worked in the Kielce region, where he converted the castles of Pińczów and Janowiec.

Sepulchral architecture was probably the most important decorative art of the time and the greatest native craftsman was Jan Michałowicz, whose superb tombs include Bishop Zebrzydowski's in Kraków (1560–65). He represented an anticlassical trend that treated architectural elements as decorative motifs. The compositional schemes were freely embellished and the niches crowned with decoration. Michałowicz was also an architect who designed the Padniewski and Zebrzydowski family chapels in

the Wawel's cathedral, examples that show how inseparably architecture and sculpture were connected in Renaissance Poland.

Painting remained the poor relation. In the Middle Ages there had been several regional schools, admittedly mostly dominated by foreigners, but throughout the sixteenth century Poland had failed to produce any outstanding painters, with the exception of the miniaturist Stanisław Samostrzelnik. Royal patronage of painting was minimal although Zygmunt August did have enthusiasms for goldsmithery and weaving. His tapestry collection, the famous *Wawel Arrases*, was rated among the best in Europe. Few of the magnates and fewer of the *szlachta* exhibited a comparable zeal for collecting; instead their taste was for objects—weapons, clothes, jewels, saddlery—that could be used for opulent public display.

Enormous disparities of wealth existed, indeed grew, in sixteenth-century Poland, and as a class the *szlachta* generally became much richer. During the century the price of the agricultural produce from their lands more than tripled and their buying power increased commensurately. At the apex, a few score of great landowning families, usually with estates in the eastern provinces, became vastly rich. The Ostrogskis possessed a hundred towns and castles, over twelve hundred villages, and an income reputed to exceed the state's revenue. This wealth was not necessarily inherited: Jan Zamoyski started with a small estate in 1571 and within thirty years controlled over eleven thousand square miles, a large amount of which he owned outright.

During this period more of the *szlachta*, both Catholic and Protestant, began to study abroad, especially in Italy—indeed Poles regularly made up a quarter of the student body at Padua University. Travel was often mixed with studies, and many returned home with foreign objects and foreign tastes. The Renaissance rediscovery of ancient Rome, which provided apparent analogies to their own nation, made a strong impression on them. So later did the myth of Sarmatism, which claimed that they alone had descended from a mysterious warrior caste that sprang from the steppes near the Black Sea—an origin that neatly distinguished them from the rest of the native population.

With these sorts of convictions, and this sort of wealth, it is hardly surprising that the *szlachta* held the real levers of power and dominated Poland. When the nation was left without a monarch after Zygmunt August's death in 1572, they moved to further extend their political power. The Seym of 1573 drew up two documents, the Pacta Conventa and the Acta Henriciana, to which all kings would have to swear. Although only a repetition of extant privileges, they severely limited royal power, making the monarch into the commonwealth's chief executive. The ambitious young deputy Zamoyski then forced a measure through the Seym that gave an equal vote to every member of the *szlachta* in the selection of a king, who might only be chosen from among their ranks or from a foreign ruling house. Thereafter the session proceeded remarkably smoothly and Henri de Valois, younger brother of Charles IX of France, was elected by an overwhelming majority. Reluctantly he swore to observe all the articles of the Acta Henriciana, including those regarding religious toleration, despite having just enthusiastically participated in the Saint Bartholomew's Day Massacre of the Huguenots in Paris. He arrived in Poland in midwinter, but in May 1574 his brother died and he became king of France. Within days he had absconded from the Wawel and refused all pleas to return—although, anxious to retain both crowns, he offered his younger brother as viceroy.

The throne was declared vacant and, after a hotly contested election in which the Habsburgs made a determined bid for it, Stefan Báthory, duke of Transylvania, was chosen in December 1575. Within four months he was installed, married to Zygmunt August's sister Anna Jagiellonka, and crowned. He proved a vigorous king and an able soldier, fending off threats from the Empire and Muscovy, but he reigned for only ten years and his death left the throne empty once again. After the Habsburgs had failed to assert their claims by force, the Seym elected Zygmunt Vasa, son of King John III of Sweden and a Jagellon princess. Their choice turned out to be less than satisfactory. A fanatical Catholic with a Habsburg wife, Zygmunt signed an "eternal" peace with Vienna while his Jesuit camarilla excluded all other influences and plotted to reconvert Poland. Succeeding to the Swedish crown on his father's death, he soon made himself so unpopular there that he abandoned Stockholm and was formally deposed by the Swedish parliament. As king of Poland for forty-five years, he dragged the country intermittently into war with Sweden, a policy for which the Seym felt no enthusiasm. Thus when in 1605 he presented proposals including a larger standing army plus the abolition of the Seym's lower chamber and the guarantes of religious freedom, discontent came to a head. A rival assembly of the *szlachta*, meeting at Sandomierz and led by Janusz Radziwiłł and Mikołaj Zebrzydowski, palatine of Kraków, voted his dethronement. While the royal troops stayed loyal and rapidly dispersed the rebels, no one was punished. But Poland was clearly no longer the peaceful and stable society it had been during the previous century.

The weaknesses of the Polish constitution, unwritten like that of England, were now plainly apparent. The elective monarchy only functioned when the king—the sole source of executive power and responsible for appointing the castellans, palatines, and bishops who constituted the Senate—acted in harmony with the political nation. Zygmunt III did the opposite. Likewise the Seym acted exclusively in the interests of the *szlachta*. During the sixteenth century the towns, always underrepresented, were steadily excluded from the legislative process, while the *szlachta* were barred from engaging in trade. The right of legal rebellion, unique to Poland, came into effect if the king broke his coronation oath to observe traditional rights and privileges. This was theoretically a healthy brake on tyranny, but it could all too easily become a prescription for anarchy. Similarly the *liberum veto*, the principle that no legislation could be enacted without unanimity, held the potential to paralyze the country's government in years to come.

Despite the uncertainties of the age, architecture continued to flourish. After 1575, however, the cultural picture became more diverse. By the seventeenth century the Renaissance style, even with its mannerist variations, no longer occupied the entire stage, for the baroque was already in evidence. Stefan Báthory and his queen as well as the magnates continued to convert and construct palaces and castles in the towns and the countryside, as well as numerous sepulchral chapels. Poland was now split into two artistic areas, one centering on Gdańsk and the other on Kraków, the importance of which had dwindled with the rise of rivals like Lublin or Lwów. In the former city, where the Renaissance had only appeared in mid-century, the style was enriched by mannerist influences from the Netherlands ably expounded by such architects and sculptors as Anton van Opbergen, Willem van der Blocke, and his son Abraham. They designed splendid municipal buildings as well as decoration and sculpture. Van Opbergen's Arsenal at Gdańsk (1602–05) is a masterpiece, its exterior adorned with rich decoration and shaped like burghers' gabled houses. Gates and town mansions were the hallmark of their work, usually including orderless elevations, foreporches, big mullioned windows, and stone features contrasting with the deep red brick background of the walls and gables. The Netherlandish influence was felt in Silesia, too, but only to a modified extent.

The architect Santi Gucci was the major figure in southern Poland. At Książ Wielki near Kielce he built a palatial residence for Bishop Piotr Myszkowski (1585–95). This *palazzo in fortezza* (an undefended palace within defensive walls) is mannerist in its forms, with a compact central block and rusticated walls counterbalanced by light, airy pavilions on either side connected to the main building by openwork arcades. For the first time the traditional inner courtyard was dispensed with in favor of a compact plan and regular interior layout. A vanished country house, Łobzów near Kraków, was also built by Gucci for the king, and he was probably the architect of Baranów for the Leszczyńskis. Working as a sculptor he designed many tombs in an idiosyncratic style: the completed monuments were often ferried down the Vistula to Mazovia, especially around Płock.

Eastern Poland also witnessed a burst of architectural activity. The Lublin ateliers were full of craftsmen from Como producing fine churches, particularly in the city and at Kazimierz Dolny; their decorative rib vaulting and stucco work gained national renown. They also designed delightful arcaded town houses, the surfaces of which are filled with bas-relief decoration, presented with the charm of naive popular art in which the elements are combined indiscriminately. Large castles were also built, the grandest of which was Krasiczyn near Przemyśl, constructed over twenty years for Marcin Krasicki. In 1597 Galeazzo Appiano planned a Renaissance building around a square interior courtyard with irregular galleries and arcades plus a tiny second-story loggia off the staircase. The attics were of special magnificence and the four massive towers were christened "Papal," "Royal," "Gentry," and "Divine" (the latter contained the domed chapel). Most interesting of all were the magnificent sgraffiti on the external walls depicting themes connected with Sarmatism and the Counter-Reformation. This particular element was one of the few here that reflected the influence of the baroque, although it must be remembered that the remodeling of the Royal Castle in Warsaw in pure baroque style was exactly contemporary.

The most remarkable building project of the age was undoubtedly Jan Zamoyski's creation of an entire Renaissance town, Zamość. The eminent Venetian architect Bernardo Morando was commissioned to create the ideal town in 1579, one designed to house several thousand people as a craft center and commercial entrepot close to important trade routes. Work began the next year. A walled and turreted pentagon enclosed two rectangles, one containing the main and subsidiary marketplaces, the other the residential quarter. The longitudinal axis ran from Zamoyski's palace to the central eastern tower through the marketplace and there intersected the latitudinal axis on which stood two smaller squares. On a second transverse axis stood the collegiate church and the academy. A synagogue, library, arsenal, public baths, churches for other denominations,

*Main square in the town of Zamość,
eastern Poland.*

and a sophisticated sewage system were all envisaged in the original plans. By the early seventeenth century Zamość was thriving and the main public buildings were completed, although work continued until around 1640. Other magnates tried to copy the idea but never with such success. The town survives as a unique monument to the belief the Polish upper classes still held—that it was possible to create a utopia on earth.

That concept receded steadily as the seventeenth century progressed. The vacillations of the government and the intrigues of overmighty magnates, several of whom interfered in the succession struggles in Russia, led Poland into a full-scale war. Polish troops occupied Moscow and Zygmunt's son Władysław was elected tsar by the boyars. His reign was brief, for a rival tsar, Mikhail Romanov, was elected in 1613. Nevertheless the situation remained confused, with spasmodic fighting until 1633 when Władysław formally abdicated all claims to the Muscovite throne. Thereafter, with the rest of Europe absorbed in the Thirty Years' War, Poland presented a peaceful picture, albeit an illusory one. The strains implicit in the Commonwealth had begun to show, particularly in the vast, fertile, and underpopulated Ukraine, where the heterogeneous inhabitants chafed under Polish rule. The papacy's folly in trying to win Orthodox converts into the Uniate Church, which acknowledged the supremacy of Rome, by allowing them to retain the Slavonic liturgy, the institution of married

priests, and communion in both kinds, enraged the bulk of the population. Only a few Ruthene nobles, keen to embrace Western culture, converted directly to Rome.

The Cossacks, communities of freebooting soldiers living on the Dnieper River, were also alienated by the government. In 1648 they rose in open revolt, defeated the royal troops, and, aided by their Tatar allies, ravaged the country. At that moment Władysław died, to be succeeded by his uninspiring younger brother, Jan Kazimierz, who was dominated by the Jesuits and his termagant wife, Marie-Louise de Gonzague. The Russians invaded in support of the Cossacks, then the Swedes attacked from the Baltic, and Lithuania seceded. By 1655 the Commonwealth appeared to have fallen apart, although a few cities held out. At last the king launched a counteroffensive. After years of warfare, peace heralded a return to the status quo except in the Ukraine, which was divided between Poland and the tsar. But Poland was left lastingly impoverished, exhausted, and in a much weaker position vis-a-vis Russia and Turkey.

The society had also become less tolerant. The advance of the Counter-Reformation meant that by the late seventeenth century admission to the ranks of the *szlachta* was restricted to Catholics. While freedom of personal religion remained, sects like the Arians and Quakers were banned and the Protestant population dwindled. The number of monasteries soared, however, and new ascetic orders were founded. The dynamic Jesuits, in the vanguard of reconversion here and across Europe, opened colleges throughout the Commonwealth and slowly forced the closure of such rival institutions as the Arian Academy of Leszno founded by the Leszczyński family. Although their artistic patronage was notable, especially in the fields of painting and architecture, the Jesuits contributed to the ossification of thought by rejecting any ideas that did not conform with their dogma. In their propaganda they skillfully portrayed Poland as the defender of Christendom against Turks and Tatars. The religious fervor they instilled made for fine soldiers, particularly among the Husaria, the famous winged cavalry. In Polish armies the latter outnumbered the infantry by three to one.

Disparities in wealth among the *szlachta* increased as grain prices dropped, exports diminished, and an agrarian recession began. In Wielkopolska many managed to hang on to their fairly small estates but elsewhere bankruptcy loomed and often they took service with one of the great magnates. A new oligarchy emerged as magnates like the Potockis, Lubomirskis, and Zamoyskis grew ever richer and more powerful, monopolizing the offices of state. In Lithuania, where the *szlachta* had always been politically immature, the situation was still worse. Frequently the newly impoverished became introspective, disinterested in advances in the outside world and convinced of the superiority of a bucolic country life close to God and nature. With many of the *szlachta* bothering less about national politics than petty local issues, the Seym lost all coherence. During the seventeenth century the Poles came to resemble their historic adversaries, the Turks, in many of their habits, costumes, and hairstyles; they even came to appreciate Islamic art. In their love of extravagance and ceremony, which they derived from their imaginary Sarmatian origins, they resembled the Ottomans. All surplus money was put into moveable property, pictures, tapestry, and statuary, which could and did suffer terribly from looting during wartime. The magnates maintained small courts, moved about the country with enormous retinues, and ignored the government's decrees when they chose. More and more the Commonwealth's exotic east/west synthesis seemed alien to the mercantilist world of Western Europe.

Poland's economic situation worsened steadily during the seventeenth century. With its economy dependent on agriculture and the export of raw materials, it was vulnerable to any slump in demand from overseas,

Portrait of Stanisław Herakliusz Lubomirski, probably by Ádám Mányoki, late seventeenth century. (Łazienki collection.)

although its import of "colonial" or finished goods was rising. The wars in mid-century had taken a heavy toll on the population, which was markedly lower in 1660 than in 1600. Larger cities had lost up to two-thirds of their inhabitants and much arable land was lying fallow. The Vasa kings only bothered intermittently with economic development. Minimal taxation meant that the most productive areas escaped proper assessment altogether and the national revenues amounted to barely one-tenth those of France. Economic retrenchment was impossible, however, for it presupposed political reform, which the ruling class rejected out of hand. Without the normal dynastic continuity the crown lacked a real power base to force through change, had the desire for it even existed.

Against this sorry slide toward decline, the Poles managed a last fine flourish. The ailing Jan Kazimierz, his queen deceased, abdicated in 1667 and retired to France. An aristocratic nonentity was elected in his place and the Turks mounted two huge invasions, conquering all of Podolia and the Ukraine. The crisis of the hour produced the man. After the Seym had voted enough money for fifty thousand soldiers, their commander-in-chief or hetman Jan Sobieski led them into battle at Chocim in 1673 and annihilated the Ottoman armies. The next year he was elected king and Poland had a vigorous ruler again. Publicly honest and pious, he was also cynical, greedy, and ambitious, yet a brilliant soldier and a capable politician. A true Sarmatian noble, he loved all things Oriental despite a lifetime spent fighting the infidel. At the same time he was a man of cosmopolitan tastes, living in an Italianate palace and marrying a French wife. Sobieski realized that a successful foreign policy would restore national prestige. Although he failed to thwart Prussian expansion, he gained European renown by raising the Turkish siege of Vienna in 1683 and routing their army. But the jealousy of his fellow-magnates undermined his

Statue of King Jan Sobieski trampling the Turks,
late seventeenth century. (Wilanów collection.)

position and frustrated his aims. Ill and apathetic, he died in 1696 and the Polish ship of state was left drifting dangerously rudderless.

It is frequently remarked that a country's artistic health has little to do with its political well-being, an observation that certainly holds for Poland, both in the seventeenth century and thereafter. True enough, the country's golden age had passed, but it was succeeded, the optimists contended, by a silver age. This was the era of baroque architecture, the final traces of which were only to fade two centuries later. Three trends had coalesced to produce the Polish baroque: the Italianate art of the Counter-Reformation, imported by the Jesuit and Carmelite orders and patronized by the court and the magnates; the humanism of the Netherlands, which fostered an interest in man and his environment and mainly influenced urban building; and the new artistic forms and motifs developed by the provincial guilds of craftsmen.

The first baroque building in Poland was the church at Nieśwież, which the Radziwiłłs commissioned from Giovanni Maria Bernardoni in 1584 with many similarities to Vignola's Gesù in Rome. It was quickly followed by others in Lublin, Lwów, Kraków, and Warsaw. Their striking use of space emphasized the simple interiors under a vast cupola with a strongly-lit apse, which gave wonderful visibility as well as excellent acoustics to the nave. Royal patronage was soon forthcoming: when the north residential wing of the Wawel burned down in 1595, Zygmunt III ordered it to be rebuilt in the baroque style, entrusting the work to the court architect, Giovanni Trevano, from Lugano. At the king's request the portals, window frames, and fireplaces were all constructed of brown marble, the staple material used during his reign. Trevano eschewed all ornament, relying for effect on his stark powerful architecture.

When the king decided to move the capital from Kraków to Warsaw in 1597, he wanted a new residence built on the site of a small medieval fortress. The resulting Royal Castle by the chief court architect, Matteo Castelli, took twenty years to complete. A notably austere edifice with a total absence of decoration and elevations interrupted only by discreet moldings, the irregular five-winged structure was designed around a dominant clock-tower with an exuberant baroque spire, which, with its corner turrets, recalled medieval Polish traditions. A glamorous court life evolved there by degrees; indeed touring companies of English actors regularly visited to present the plays of Shakespeare and Marlowe. In the 1620s Castelli designed an equally massive summer palace for Zygmunt at nearby Ujazdów, which, with octagonal turrets at each corner, harked back to Gothic precedents. It did contain some innovations, however, including the triple arcaded loggia overlooking the Vistula River as well as a tall sloping roof unconcealed by an attic.

It did not take long for the magnates to adopt the prevailing style. For Stanisław Lubomirski, palatine of Kraków and prince of the Holy Roman Empire whose father had made the family's fortune as commissioner for the salt mines, Matteo Trapola built the castle of Łańcut and from 1615 onward reconstructed that of Nowy Wiśnicz in Małopolska. The latter, strategically placed on a hill, was extended to a massive three-story rectangle surrounded by a bastioned pentagonal wall and approached through a showy main gate ornamented with scrolls and banded masonry. The interior housed a court of up to two hundred, a large staff, and a permanent garrison. An elegant arcaded loggia was added to the courtyard and the chapel was redesigned to be tall and narrow with an ornate gallery. Some of the period's buildings were less harmonious; the bishop of Kraków's new summer palace at Kielce appears curiously heavy with its twin towers theatrically joined to the main block and the enormous castle of Podhorce in Podolia, built for the Koniecpolskis in the 1630s, was more a fortress than a residence. Counter-Reformation piety inspired other kinds of building, too, such as the pilgrimage site at Kalwaria west of Kraków, begun

Distant view of Nowy Wiśnicz, southern Poland.

after 1600 by the Zebrzydowskis. There, an entire hillside was covered with chapels and monuments.

By mid-century Poland had a reasonably uniform baroque, both in architecture and in painting, where the Venetian school, which produced monumental canvases, fused with that of the Flemish portrait painters' followers to produce a stream of pictures in the Sarmatian style, often more iconography than art. As Warsaw gained artistic supremacy the standardization that resulted led to a decline in the importance of the provincial centers. Refined linear construction employing concave panels and flat pilasters epitomized the period's buildings. The monumental castle of Krzyżtopór was typical. Built for Krzysztof Ossoliński, it consisted of a number of courtyards set on sprawling star-shaped fortifications and radiating from a central cour d'honneur. Fashionable black Dębnik marble was used for plaques over the windows, which carried Latin inscriptions, and for the magnificent baroque rebus over the main gate depicting a crucifix and an axe, the family coat of arms. It took thirteen years to complete this gigantic stage set but its life was sadly brief: Krzyżtopór was gutted by the Swedes in 1655 and never rebuilt.

Fortunately baroque architecture was to be reinvigorated by a man of remarkable talents, Tylman van Gameren. Born in Utrecht in 1632, he arrived in Poland at the age of thirty-four at the invitation of Stanisław Herakliusz Lubomirski, a young man married to an intellectual wife who fancied himself a writer-philosopher. Tylman was to take Polish citizenship and the name Gamerski. After the havoc caused by the Swedish invasions in the mid-seventeenth century, Warsaw had to be substantially rebuilt, and Tylman, with his patron, largely dictated artistic taste in the transformed capital. Emphasizing contour, simplicity, and restraint as elements of "harmonious" art, he soon became the most sought-after architect. For Lubomirski he designed a garden pavilion in the Ujazdów Park with a bathhouse that one day would be turned into the Łazienki Palace. He also created two less successful bigger houses, Puławy and the grandest of all, Łubnice, since totally destroyed. Beside the Vistula he may also have built the delightful Otwock Stary for the Bielińskis, a house with exquisite red stucco reliefs, urns and trophies, broken pediments over the windows, and a garlanded Bacchanal on the central tympanum, influenced more perhaps by French than Dutch taste. Grabki Duże, an especially charming house built under his influence in Małopolska, was designed for a diplomat who had returned from Turkey, with four miniature pavilions linked by a hall under a swirling octagon.

As king, Jan Sobieski favored the baroque as well, commissioning a summer palace for himself in 1677 on land he had bought at Wilanów just outside the capital. More and more aristocratic residences rose in Warsaw, the majority constructed by Tylman. Although the Morsztyn and Ossoliński palaces have been lost, the small Ostrogski and the splendid Krasiński palaces still survive, the latter's elevation adorned with an order of colossal pilasters. Not all of the seventy-five secular and ecclesiastical buildings attributed to Tylman were of an equally high standard. And the quality of work produced by the so-called Wilno and Kraków Schools, with their emotive and restless aesthetic, which appealed primarily to the spectator's feelings, was extremely uneven. It was reassuring, however, that the embattled Commonwealth could go on begetting such a profusion of fine buildings despite the succession of political disasters it endured.

The Seym of 1697 was a dismal affair, aptly illustrating the nation's decay. Although a French candidate had been chosen to succeed Sobieski, who had died the year before, the rival candidate Friedrich Augustus, elector of Saxony, seized the throne and was crowned as Augustus II,

View from across the garden of Otwock Stary, near Warsaw.

nicknamed the Strong. The epithet applied more to his physique and virility than to his intellect. He dreamed of turning Poland into an absolutist monarchy and in alliance with Peter the Great promptly embroiled his new subjects in war with Sweden. When the Russians were routed at the Battle of Narva, Augustus tried to sue for peace, but the Swedes were not so easily pacified. First invading Saxony and demanding the king's dethronement, they then arranged another "election" with an assembly of compliant *szlachta* and proclaimed the Palatine of Poznań, Stanisław Leszczyński, king of Poland in 1704. His rule was short-lived, however, for when the Swedes were defeated at Poltava five years later Augustus reascended the Polish throne. He had been immeasurably weakened in the process and was now practically a Russian puppet. When the king reached an impasse with the Seym, for instance, the tsar's envoy arrived in Warsaw in 1715 with eighteen thousand troops to maintain order. The rising power of Prussia displayed a similar disregard for Poland's pretensions—the elector of Brandenburg now styled himself "king in Prussia," although the duchy was still notionally a vassal of the Commonwealth.

Augustus's death from alcohol poisoning in 1733 was accompanied by the immortal words, "My whole life has been one uninterrupted sin. God have mercy on me." The thirteen thousand electors gathered in Warsaw unanimously voted for Leszczyński, but Russia, Austria, and Prussia thought otherwise. They had decided that the king's son, another Augustus, should succeed, and with a small assembly of overawed *szlachta* they arranged matters accordingly. Their presumption did not go uncontested, for Louis XV of France was Stanisław's son-in-law, and forthwith began the War of the Polish Succession. Two years of sporadic fighting accomplished nothing and Leszczyński was compensated with the duchy of Lorraine. Augustus III soon proved himself an indolent disaster. His reign was to last three decades, only a fraction of which he spent in Poland. Since he did nothing to curtail their privileges he was not unpopular with the *szlachta*. Indeed Polish constitutional liberties, especially the *liberum veto*, which could be used to thwart the passage of any legislation through the Seym, were zealously protected by the neighboring governments who well knew they were the safest way to perpetuate anarchy. The country was run by a handful of magnate families whose good offices were courted by half of Europe.

Disparities of wealth had grown further by the mid-eighteenth century. The war against Sweden had done immense damage. Agricultural prices continued to fall while yields increased a negligible amount in marked contrast to Western Europe. Most of the peasantry and the lesser *szlachta* experienced a decline in their standard of living; indeed a large proportion of the latter now owned no land at all. Poorly educated and chiefly preoccupied with the chase, military service, the sale of agrarian produce, and lawsuits with their neighbors, they bore little resemblance to the image of the cultivated Polish gentleman of two centuries before. Although serfdom in the Russian sense was unknown in the Commonwealth, the peasants, except for a significant number of small freeholders, were tied to the land by economic necessity. And because the landowning class controlled the courts, they could exercise the power of life and death over their tenantry. Significantly, in an era of mercantile stagnation the Jewish community was the most pauperized of all.

But the magnates undeniably prospered. In eastern Poland, the proportion of land in estates of over seventy-five hundred hectares had tripled to over half of the total since the sixteenth century. In Lithuania and the Ukraine, some properties were larger than many German principalities. Luxury had become ostentatious, and frequently in questionable taste. Nieśwież, an immense ensemble of buildings constructed around a hexagonal courtyard and enclosed by a moat, had been continuously added to by the Radziwiłłs since the 1580s. Yet with its twelve great halls, seven gilt domes, and a peristyle of gilt columns, the prevailing impression was one of vulgarity. Neither was Nieśwież alone—four towers at Żółkiew Castle were covered in gilt copper and Podhorce was wrecked by clumsy eighteenth-century alterations, which coarsened the original silhouette. (Nevertheless its architectural hanging gardens on three terraces still excited admiration.) Białystok, a house designed by Tylman van Gameren for the Branickis, was enlarged by Sigismund Deybel in the 1730s into an overpowering mass, occasioning Princess Marthe Bibesco's famous jibe, "*C'était Versailles sans la Révolution française, mais aussi Versailles sans génie.*" Indeed it is recorded that while the stables held two hundred horses and the theatre could seat four hundred, the library only contained 170 books.

Whatever their shortcomings, both Saxon kings genuinely loved the arts, for it was they who turned their capital at Dresden into one of the jewels of Europe. Their sole major contribution in Poland, however, was to add a new wing to the Royal Castle in Warsaw and to refurbish it throughout. Yet thanks to their patronage, the influence of Italy in Polish architecture was superseded by that of France and the Dresden rococo. Its most distinguished exponents were Józef and Jakub Fontana, members of a Polandized dynasty of craftsmen from the Swiss canton of Ticino who had settled in the country a century before. They designed one of the most distinguished of Mazovian country houses at Radzyń Podlaski, where reconstruction for the Potockis started in 1750. Three wings framed a square courtyard: the main two-story house with a slightly higher central block and two end bays pushed subtly forward. Both of the low side wings had central gateways surmounted by towers with pilastered concave recesses topped by obelisks. The orangery was similarly muted, with nine big windows and pairs of plain Ionic columns between pilasters at either end. Radzyń Podlaski was all very French and formal, a brilliantly conceived scheme showing that the Poles were still capable of great creativity.

General view through the gates at Radzyń Podlaski, eastern Poland.

The chaos notwithstanding, rays of hope shone on the horizon. In 1747 the Załuski brothers' book collections were opened as the first public reference library in Europe, which grew to over a half-million volumes in fifty years. A few of the higher aristocracy advocated reform, led by the "Familia," the name given to the relations and supporters of the Czartoryski family, consisting of the five children of Prince Kazimierz Czartoryski's marriage to the heiress Izabela Morsztyn. One son, August, produced a boy, Adam Kazimierz, for whom royal hopes were nurtured, since the family descended from the Jagellons. A daughter married a man of humble *szlachta* origins, Stanisław Poniatowski, who became an accomplished soldier and diplomat. They too produced a son named Stanisław. Carefully brought up and widely traveled, he settled in Saint Petersburg in 1755 and there became the new lover of Grand Duchess Catherine. It was a friendship that was to stand him in good stead. Her seizure of the Russian throne seven years later just preceded the death of Augustus III. When the Seym met to choose a new king the tsarina let it be known that she would have no objections to the election of her former paramour, who happened to be the Familia's candidate anyway. He was duly chosen in 1764, taking the name of Stanisław II August.

Reforms were initiated immediately. Among measures placed before the Confederated Seym (so-called because it could now pass legislation by majority vote) were the establishment of fiscal and military commissions, a national customs tariff, and a state academy for training public servants. Majority voting was made mandatory for the provincial seyms as well. When the abolition of the *liberum veto* was proposed, however, the reaction from Russia and Prussia was explosive. Not only did they demand the invariable observation of Poland's traditional constitutional liberties, which negated any prospect of reforms, but they also called for full civic rights for their particular religious minorities, the Eastern Orthodox and the Lutherans. While the king and the Seym bowed to such irresistible pressure, others did not. An organization called the Confederation of Bar, a strange mixture of reactionary magnates and liberal idealists, declared the dethronement of Stanisław August and started a civil war. But the Russians quickly crushed the rebels, five thousand of whom were deported to Siberia.

Using the insurrection as an excuse, Frederick the Great persuaded Russia and Austria to join with Prussia in the First Partition of Poland in 1772. The three powers took about 30 percent of Polish territory and 35 percent of the population. Alarmed by the public outcry this evoked, they forced the Seym to rubber-stamp this fait accompli and the country subsided in outraged impotence. Yet curiously it engendered an amazing renewal in the political life of the nation. For the next sixteen years the remaining Poles were governed by the Permanent Council, effectively the first modern administration they had ever had. The dissolution of the Jesuit Order in 1771 handed over fifty colleges, twenty thousand pupils, and substantial properties to the state, which proceeded to set up a commission for national education to supervise the schools and overhaul the universities. Extensive legal changes were proposed, although not adopted in the end.

Acknowledging that political reform was unattainable, Stanisław August played an enormous role in encouraging the intellectual revival. He founded the *Monitor*, a weekly journal modeled on England's *Spectator*, set up a national theatre, promoted writers and poets, brought foreign composers like Giovanni Paesiello and Domenico Cimarosa to Warsaw, thereby resuscitating a musical tradition vibrant in Poland since the fourteenth century, and patronized art and architecture on a grand scale. Sadly his dream of founding academies of science and of fine arts as well as the Museum Polonicum were never realized. But he spent a fortune on his scheme for he sincerely believed that his cultural legacy was to inspire future generations with a vision of an enlightened nation. Nor were his efforts in vain. By 1780 a Polish intelligentsia could definitely be said to exist and various enlightened magnates followed his lead, including Stanisław Lubomirski, Ignacy Potocki, and Andrzej Zamoyski. A few began to set up factories, dig canals, foster industrialization, even found banks. Trade slowly revived and the urban population grew, even as the law forbidding the *szlachta* to engage in commerce was repealed.

But the Familia, joined by members of the Potocki and Lubomirski clans, had turned against the king. Without personal wealth, he relied on his natural charm and intelligence plus the advantages of his position. Cultured, cosmopolitan, and patriotic, he was nevertheless no hero and, in need of support, turned once more to the Russians. Unfortunately his meeting with Catherine in 1787 was not a success, for she disdainfully rejected his proffered help in her Turkish war. The following year the "Great Seym" met and, with Stanisław August's stature so reduced, took matters into its own hands. An increase in the size of the army was voted, funded for the first time by a land tax of 10 percent for the *szlachta* and 20 percent for the Church. The Permanent Council was abolished and a commission was appointed to draft a written constitution. The radicals pressed for more drastic reforms and, against the background of the French Revolution, introduced proposals to make the Seym into the chief legislative and executive power to whom the king and ministers would be answerable. The veto was abolished and far-reaching economic changes discussed.

Catherine did not hesitate. Alarmed by this evidence of revolutionary fervor, she lined up Austrian and Prussian support and in 1792 a large Russian army invaded. Resistance was obviously futile and Stanisław August hastened to submit. But it was to no avail: the next year the powers signed a Second Partition of Poland under which three-fifths of the country was annexed, leaving the non-viable rump of a buffer state with a population of four million. Although the Seym was browbeaten into ratification, revolt was inevitable. In 1794 it broke out in Kraków, where the heroic Tadeusz Kościuszko defeated the Russian troops. Warsaw rose as well, and the garrison retreated from the city. But the insurrection could only have one outcome. Within six months all resistance had been crushed, the king was removed to Saint Petersburg, and in 1795 the Third Partition wiped Poland off the map.

Architectural evolution in the later eighteenth century was almost as dramatic as the political. The neoclassical style arrived in the country around 1760, mainly through French influence, although England also contributed much to a movement that included architecture, decorative art, painting, sculpture, and garden design. At the start neoclassicism coexisted with the decaying baroque and rococo, and later with the romanticizing strains of the neo-Gothic. For its proponents, Greek art was considered the ideal reflection of the philosophy of the Enlightenment. The style was meant to follow designated rules and instructions, to be linear rather than freely inventive, simple in form and restrained in decoration. Magnates like the Czartoryskis and Branickis had already brought back textiles and objets d'art from Paris in the new fashion, and interest in classical architecture such as that depicted in Piranesi's engravings was growing—at least ten Poles were studying it on the spot in Italy. But it was Stanisław August's active patronage that established neoclassicism in Poland.

By the time Augustus III died, the Royal Castle in Warsaw was half ruined and its reconstruction became one of the new regime's most urgent tasks. Under the supervision of Jakub Fontana, work began on the creation of a series of official halls with an impressive facade facing the old town, and of such cultural focal points as a theatre, library, and picture gallery. Plans were commissioned from the French architect Victor Louis

Portrait of Marie Walewska by François Gérard, early nineteenth century. (Polish National Portrait Collection, Wilanów.)

Pompeian-style decoration at Mała Wieś, central Poland.

in Paris, but were substantially abandoned on grounds of expense. With a shortage of materials and craftsmen in Poland, it was said to cost as much to build a brick palace in Warsaw as a marble one in Rome. Work was delayed by a bad fire in 1767, although it soon recommenced under the direction of the official court architect, Domenico Merlini, a pupil of the Fontanas, in partnership with the talented interior designer Jan Chrystian Kamsetzer. Improvements and extensions to the original plans continued until 1786 when the king decided to concentrate his severely reduced funds and aspirations entirely on the Ujazdów estate, which he had bought from the Lubomirskis on his accession.

Stanisław August's patronage also extended to painting. He invited many foreign artists to Warsaw: Marcello Bacciarelli, who set up his studio in the Royal Castle; Canaletto's nephew, Bernardo Bellotto, who became the official court painter for twelve years until his death in 1780 and produced a stream of city and architectural views. His example was to be followed by Zygmunt Vogel, and in the nineteenth century by Marcin Zaleski. Both the king and magnates patronized such portraitists as Giovanni Battista Lampi, Angelica Kauffmann, and Marie-Louise-Elizabeth Vigée-Lebrun, and Polish artists were sponsored to study abroad. Franciszek, Smuglewicz became a successful painter of historical and genre subjects; Aleksander Kucharski developed into a fashionable portrait painter. So the foundations were laid for the solid achievements of the Romantic School in Poland during the next century.

The major changes in Poland's economic and intellectual life began to be reflected by the mid-1770s in new architectural concepts. A house designed by Efraim Szreger for the banker Piotr Fergusson Tepper was intended to be both an office and a home divided into apartments, the first of several similar urban dwellings. Both Szreger and Szymon Bogumił Zug created buildings for a variety of purposes in their own neoclassical idioms. Zug built a number of town halls, a hotel, and even a well-head in Warsaw. Stanisław Zawadzki specialized in military construction, especially of barracks. A typically Polish mansion reflecting national taste evolved by this time, particularly in the countryside—a one- or two-storied building set into the surrounding landscape. Good examples of this were Walewice (future home of Napoleon's inamorata, Marie Walewska) and Mała Wieś, both designed with rectangular layouts by Hilary Szpilowski in the 1780s. The latter also had excellent stucco work and very fine murals.

Italian influences on patrons and architects remained important, particularly the influence of Palladio. The work of Chrystian Piotr Aigner best represented this trend although Merlini's villa of Królikarnia and Zawadzki's of Lubostroń were both broadly modeled on the Villa Rotonda. Many Polish houses had their *corps de logis* linked to wings by a variety of galleries: semicircular, elliptical, refracted at right angles, or even straight. While Palladio's galleries were open rows of pillars, the majority here were closed and arcaded. So popular did this style become that forty such buildings were constructed from 1775 to 1800. Their monumental appearance concealed utilitarian advantages in the siting of bedroom and service quadrangles. In the later works of Zug and Szreger, an avant-garde trend was discernible based on juxtaposing geometric solids, and using minimal decoration, rusticated surfaces, and the Doric order; but at first this was confined to church design.

Architectural developments in Wielkopolska during the eighteenth century well illustrate the course of events in all of Poland. Except for the Leszczyńskis (until King Stanisław's exile in France) and the Sułkowskis, favorites of the Saxon kings, there were no magnate familes of wealth equivalent to their peers elsewhere. But the *szlachta's* estates were the best run in Poland, with more intensive agriculture and higher yields, better sheep breeding, and a certain amount of nascent industry. Since Sobieski's reign there had been much building activity—these years produced Pompeo Ferrari's Rydzyna, a grand aristocratic residence integrated into the town, which he designed for the Leszczyńskis. The local style predominated: a great room placed on the house's main axis across its entire breadth with a simply built staircase parallel to the facade. The marked influence of Austrian baroque was shown in the rich, high cornices.

Evidence of the shift of taste in mid-century may be found in Rogalin. Initially conceived in Viennese taste around 1770, a severer style prevailed with only six plain Ionic pilasters on the front facade. The curved orderless wings of 1782 joining up the flanking pavilions are definitely of English inspiration, but Kamsetzer's internal work from six years later was mainstream neoclassical. The final touch was provided by the picturesque Roman-style chapel built beside the road in 1820 and based on the *Maison Carrée* at Nimes. The Silesian architect Karl Gothard Langhans was the first to introduce the English style to Wielkopolska; his best country-house was Pawłowice (1779–83), which he designed with big Ionic columns under a straight architrave crowned by statues and a flat mansard roof. Pilastered quarter-circle galleries connected to elegant side-pavilions. Internally Kamsetzer enlarged the circular salon in 1789, adding two rectangular bays and twenty-four freestanding Corinthian columns to create a room as grandiose as any in Warsaw's Royal Castle. Other houses, however, were more in the French taste, such as Lewków, its elevations charmingly overornamented with painted and sculpted plaster-work, or the more splendid Czerniejewo, which boasted a massive portico and two circular halls one above the other. Merlini's Racot was simple in design while Zawadzki's Śmiełów from the 1790s was more elaborate. The main facade of the latter was enriched by an Ionic columned portico combined with pilasters of the same order and trophies on the end bays, while the pavilions had entrances framed by sunken Doric pillars, triglyph friezes, and ingenious two-stage roofs.

After 1780, as the ideals of Romanticism succeeded the baroque, smaller country houses, more like villas or *maisons de plaisance*, came into vogue,

Neoclassical chapel at Rogalin, western Poland.

Rogalin seen from across the garden.

epitomizing the wish for a more intimate and family-oriented lifestyle. Delicate white stucco decor blending with pale marbled walls were contrasted with Pompeian red, the favourite color, while gold disappeared completely. Zug's first commission from Izabela Lubomirska was Natolin near Warsaw, begun in 1780 and known as the "Bażantarnia" (Pheasantry). No portico crowned the entrance and the oval salon opened onto the garden. The courtyard lay between two long projecting wings. Natolin mixed French and English ideas; the oval peristyle, an element propounded by Sir William Chambers, blended with the form and proportions of the windows drawn from Neufforge's *Receuil elementaire d'architecture*. Merlini's Jabłonna, built for the king's brother, Michał Poniatowski, the primate of Poland, was even simpler: a circular ballroom within square walls projects onto the terrace. The house was roofed by a cupola concealed in a belvedere and the octagonal drum thus formed was surmounted by a baroque spire bearing a globe.

From the start neoclassicism was accompanied by ideas of landscape emanating from England and partially derived from China. These arrived in Poland around 1770 via Chambers's writings and the designs Capability Brown made for Catherine the Great. According to landscape theorists the park should imitate nature in all its asymmetrical irregularities. With serene landscapes to represent beautiful nature, melancholy ones to evoke wild nature, and surprising ones to attract the spectator's attention, the aim was to create the picturesque. The park should contain inscriptions on patriotic or humanist themes and ideally should be separated from its surroundings by a ditch rather than a wall. In this private domain freedom, not reason, ruled. In 1774, however, the first Polish treatise on landscape design appeared. Written by August Moszyński, it was intended to influence the king's projects but it sensibly described the Warsaw area as largely unsuitable for such schemes, being too flat and monotonous except for the Vistula escarpment.

Architects like Zug were already converted to these theories and soon began to put them into practice. The first Polish landscape park was designed at Powązki by its owner Izabella Czartoryska, who would later lay out the most famous park of them all at Puławy. With the help of the French painter Jean-Pierre Norblin, she created an escapist paradise. It was quickly copied at Siedlce, where Zawadzki was commissioned by the Ogińskis to remodel the house and park. Zug was simultaneously embarking on the landscape at Mokotów in the suburbs of Warsaw for Izabela Lubomirska. In 1778 he started work at Arkadia for Helena Radziwiłł, the park that would survive as his masterpiece. The fashion later spread to Volhynia and the Ukraine where an Irishman known as Dionizy McClaire laid out many landscapes, the best known being on the Potockis' estate at Zofiówka. Great ingenuity was shown in using all features of the terrain, in establishing surprising vistas, and in producing unusual combinations of vegetation and architecture. The decorative and architectural motifs employed were extremely varied: temples, ruins, triumphal arches, aqueducts, obelisks, altars, urns, and sarcophagi. From the classical world, amphitheatres were borrowed; from the Chinese, pagodas and bridges; from the Turkish, kiosks and minarets. Neo-Gothic follies, hermitages, sham castles, and grottoes were mixed together with orangeries and aviaries, and a rustic touch was provided by shepherds' cottages, mills, and cow-barns. Monuments of all kind became a feature of Polish landscape architecture, dedicated to the patriotic cult.

Patriotism was a virtue of which the Poles stood much in need at the close of the eighteenth century. However, many had no intention of submitting tamely to their nation's extinction. Under French auspices a regular army commanded by Jan Henryk Dąbrowski was formed in 1797, bearing the proud motto "Poland is not yet lost so long as we are alive." Despite its apparent support, France consistently failed the Polish cause, which it abandoned whenever convenient at successive peace treaties. Yet Napoleon captured the imagination of a people forced by circumstance to desire the overthrow of the established European order. In 1806 Bonaparte's troops entered Poznań and Dąbrowski was allowed to issue a call to insurrection. A triumphal entry into Warsaw ensued with patriots donating their plate and jewelry to the national cause. After Napoleon and Tsar Alexander I met at Tilsit, it was agreed the duchy of Warsaw should be formed from the territory seized by Prussia. Eminent Poles served in its government, including Józef Poniatowski, the last king's nephew, who became commander-in-chief and war minister. The French blatantly exploited the duchy, which actually went bankrupt, but they did not forfeit the country's affections. In 1812, on the eve of Napoleon's invasion of Russia, ninety-eight thousand men, the largest foreign contingent, joined the Grande Armée and performed prodigies of valor during the campaign; three-quarters of them never returned.

The victorious allies showed clemency. Urged by Adam Jerzy Czartoryski, his intimate friend and adviser, Tsar Alexander I suggested the formation of a Polish state under the Russian sceptre. What emerged from the Congress of Vienna was a country of almost eighty thousand square miles carved out of all three partitions—the so-called Congress Kingdom. Although the tsar's brother Grand Duke Constantine was installed at Warsaw to command the army, Czartoryski's constitution was the most liberal in Central Europe. In this congenial cultural climate, education flourished: the University of Wilno became a center of academic life, the Zamoyski and Czartoryski libraries were opened to the public, and the late-eighteenth-century revival continued. However Alexander soon tired of his liberal experiment. The Seym was dissolved in 1820 and over the

Marshal Prince Józef Poniatowski by Frantisek Paderewski, early nineteenth century. (Polish National Portrait Collection, Wilanów.)

View from across the park of Pawłowice, western Poland.

next decade the Congress Kingdom's theoretical liberties were steadily eroded.

His successor, Nicholas I, hated all dissent, so when the Poles rose in 1830 in the wake of the revolution in France he demanded unconditional surrender. The Seym voted his dethronement and Czartoryski headed an independent government. But it did not last long. Polish military incompetence, Czartoryski's fatal indecision, and the lack of any material support from the western powers facilitated the task of the huge invading Russian army. Warsaw was stormed, the remaining rebels seeking refuge in Austrian or Prussian territory. Retribution was brutal—the constitution was abolished, many families had their estates confiscated, ten thousand officers were deported to Russia, and the universities were closed. Even the fiction of an independent Poland vanished once more for nearly a century.

It is a tribute to Polish resilience that the three partitions of the country affected its art and architecture relatively little. Naturally the loss of royal patronage was felt, especially in the territories annexed by the Austrians and Prussians where the infiltration of government-sponsored artists was resented. But Stanisław August's achievement had been to create a large group of artists, Polish by origin or naturalization, who now formed part of the urban intelligentsia and who were involved in the struggle to maintain the national identity. Neoclassical painting and architecture continued to flourish until 1830, although the neo-Gothic had appeared in the preceding decade. Admittedly until 1815 there were few construction projects in the big cities, but this was balanced by a growth in rural building, including smaller country houses. After the creation of the Congress Kingdom, the foundation of an industrial dimension to the economy brought a need for new approaches to planning and architecture—medieval town ramparts, for instance, needed to be destroyed to make way for wide thoroughfares. And with the reestablishment of a national capital adding to the revival of state patronage, an enormous boost was given to the development of Polish architecture.

In Wielkopolska, which stayed in Prussian hands throughout this period, the country houses of Lubostroń and Pawłowice were both completed after the final partition. By degrees some magnates even turned to Berlin for ideas. In 1822 Karl Friedrich Schinkel designed the hunting lodge at Antonin for the Radziwiłłs. There, four three-story wings under steep gables radiated from an octagon; inside, a central hall rising the height of the house and centered on an enormous stove was surrounded by galleries, off which led smaller rooms. In 1834, Tytus Działyński remodeled his moated house at Kórnik following Schinkel's gothicizing plans, which were very different from his usual neoclassical edifices. Gradually he turned it into an arcaded, machicolated, and turreted Gothic castle. The entrance hall was star-vaulted while another hall had three-dimensional rib vaulting with elaborate capitals. Other buildings were still in pure neoclassical style, such as Białaczów in Małopolska, begun in 1800 on the grand scale by the prolific architect Jakub Kubicki. The main block has an imposing portico on its southern facade and a projecting octagonal salon on its northern. Natolin, too, was remodeled by Chrystian Piotr Aigner in the early 1800s at the behest of its owners, Aleksander and Anna Potocki, who also had a large landscape in the English style laid out there. Jabłonna, too, the property of Anna Potocka, was similarly remodeled and a monument was later erected to the heroic Józef Poniatowski, drowned while covering Napoleon's retreat at the Battle of Leipzig. At Puławy, Izabella Czartoryska was busy transforming the park into a shrine to Polish patriotism.

With the birth of the Congress Kingdom, older architects like Aigner,

Main facade of Smiełów, western Poland.

in his seventies, and Kubicki, nearly sixty, recommenced work. Possibly according to Aigner's plans, the Krasińskis had a delightful neo-Gothic house built at Opinogóra in which a suite of rib-vaulted rooms lead to an octagonal corner tower. The older architects were soon joined by two young Italians, Antonio Corazzi and Enrico Marconi. The former was to spend twenty-seven years in Poland working mainly in the towns and for the government; the latter was to play a major role in country-house building, marrying a Scotswoman and producing two sons who, after his death in 1863, continued his practice until 1914. Corazzi contributed four monumental buildings to Warsaw, which breathed a romantic element into the neoclassical movement.

One symbol of continuity was provided by the painter Marcello Bacciarelli, who had become a sort of director-general of fine arts for Stanisław August and outlived his patron by almost two decades. Until his death in 1817, his atelier in the Royal Castle continued to function as something of a private business. The theme of history painting was taken up by Franciszek Smuglewicz's numerous pupils, who often alluded to current events with their classical subjects and stressed the attributes of a virtuous life: simplicity, sacrifice, and patriotism.

These were qualities needed by the Poles in the nineteenth century. Tsar Nicholas, who decreed Russian to be the official language, ruled Poland as a defeated enemy country. Not surprisingly the people regularly rebelled, in 1846 and again in 1848, "The Year of Revolutions," when the desperate Prussians and Austrians did make initial concessions. They proved merely ephemeral. Risings in Poznań, Lwów, and Kraków were crushed and the rebels bombarded into submission. As if to vent their frustrations, many Poles fought in the revolutions abroad: three thousand under General Józef Bem joined Lajos Kossuth's Hungarian army and some even served under the Turkish banner in the Crimea. Nicholas's death made little difference, for his successor, Alexander II, was only ostensibly liberal, admonishing one deputation of his Polish subjects, "*Pas de rêveries, Messieurs!*" Some reforms were nevertheless instituted. Practical aristocrats like Aleksander Wielopolski, who despised romantic revolutionaries, persuaded the Russians by 1860 to concede a measure of administrative reform, allow the creation of consultative bodies, and ease the educational clampdown. His rival, Andrzej Zamoyski, advocated land reform and the possibility of commuting labor rents to money rents with permanent tenancies convertible into freeholds. Yet national discontent boiled over again. In 1863 an insurrection was proclaimed. Peasants and *szlachta* united and, aided by risings in Lithuania, for eighteen months defied Europe's largest army. But the struggle was to no avail—the insurgents were defeated, their leaders hanged, and intensive oppression resumed.

Only about eight thousand Poles had escaped to the west in 1831, but their importance was disproportionate to their numbers and their departure was christened "the Great Emigration." Most settled in Paris, where the conservative emigrés led by Adam Jerzy Czartoryski worked for Poland's independence through international diplomatic channels. They were encouraged by the outbreak of the Crimean War, for Napoleon III's half-Polish foreign minister was Count Alexandre Florian Walewski, the bastard son of his uncle Napoleon I by Marie Walewska. In the end, however, France and Britain bought Austrian and Prussian neutrality by burying the issue. A plethora of other emigré groups also existed, united only by their agreement on the need for national regeneration. Although its attempts were continually foiled, the most effective of these was the Democratic Society, an organization committed to fomenting mass revolution. The nearest the Poles came to having a universal spokesman was the poet Adam Mickiewicz, who for the last twenty years of his life abandoned literature to devote himself to the national cause.

*View from across the garden at Natolin,
near Warsaw.*

View of Jabłonna, near Warsaw.

Hope was not quite extinguished by mid-century. The tsar's promise, made under the pressure of revolution, to emancipate the peasants by granting them the land they tilled was subsequently honored, leaving many Poles far better off than their Russian counterparts. Yet Saint Petersburg's attack on the Catholic Church caused widespread resentment, for Catholicism and nationalism were by now inseparable. Even the traditionally reactionary minor *szlachta* were turned into fierce extremists. Those opinions were fully shared by most magnates, although some still believed in the necessity of limited cooperation with the occupying power to keep the state functioning. But gradually the nineteenth-century positivist belief in self-help and material progress mitigated the most uncompromising nationalism and fostered the notion that qualified loyalty would lead to qualified concessions. Russian protectionist policies engendered an economic boom from the 1870s and a Polish industrial revolution belatedly occurred. The agricultural picture was less rosy, for the emancipation of the peasants in 1864 had ruined many of the minor *szlachta*, forcing them to sell up and drift off into the towns. The big estates, on the other hand, were minimally affected.

The drive to Russify the Poles was paralleled by Otto von Bismarck's endeavours to Germanize them in the Prussian zone of Wielkopolska. This was perhaps the best-governed region, for if its administration was heavy-handed at least it avoided overt persecution. Attempts to buy out Polish landowners and forbid the language failed, and in industry the Poles started to take over from the Germans. Agriculture in Wielkopolska became more competitive and conditions in the villages were eased thanks to wholesale emigration to the Americas. As fellow Catholics, the Austrians should have been the most sympathetic rulers of partitioned Poland, but their bureaucratic rigidity made them averse to compromise, while they viewed their heavily-taxed province of Galicia primarily as a source of manpower and raw materials for the Empire. Indeed Galicia remained backward. Its industrial development was hampered by competition from Bohemia and its great landholdings were still operated along traditional lines. Successive military defeats made Vienna more conciliatory, however. De facto local autonomy was granted; the Poles were given their own Seym as well as an indigenous viceroy, while deputies

Park facade of Kórnik, western Poland.

Emperor Francis Joseph with Count and Countess Lancoroński on army maneuvers in Galicia, 1903. (Prince Stanisław Lubomirski.)

were elected to the Imperial Parliament. Their independent education system boasted two universities, at Lwów and Kraków.

In the Russian zone of Poland it became apparent as the twentieth century dawned that tsarist policies alternating between partial autonomy and outright incorporation had failed. The irreconcilable differences were compounded by the new tsar's disinterest in any significant changes in Poland's status, which in turn led to the revival of revolutionary activity. The Socialists (the PPS), led by Józef Piłsudski, were adept at dodging the police and conducting a terrorist campaign. With tacit Austrian approval they used Galicia as a base for their activities. They were opposed by Roman Dmowski's middle-class, anti-Semitic National Democrats, who regarded Germany rather than Russia as the chief enemy and who even participated in the tsarist Duma or parliament. The Catholic Church cleverly identified itself with no specific party and thus came to symbolize the nation. Poland's chance came with World War I. Although Piłsudski's Polish legions fought with the Austrians against the Russians, he astutely refused to become the pawn of anyone, since all three occupying powers seemed to be considering the idea of an independent Poland. The western powers were slowly persuaded to endorse this idea, too. Facilitated by the German collapse and the Russian revolution, at length it became a reality in 1918.

It is hardly surprising that Polish architecture suffered from so prolonged a loss of nationhood. At first after the final partition the neoclassical style carried on. Marconi continued to convert and design country houses in the 1830s and '40s, as well as embellish such parks as Natolin, where he constructed a Doric temple based on that at Paestum. Excellent sculptors like Paweł Maliński, Ludwik Kaufman, and Jakub Tatarkiewicz (a pupil of Bertel Thorvaldsen) continued to produce a stream of work. New architects like J. Gay and Franciszek Maria Lanci introduced the use of ironwork into their buildings in the form of columns, cornice supports, and even staircases, while the delicate elevations were ornamented with elegantly thin pilasters. But the occupying powers were not interested in promoting Polish culture, so as the generation of craftsmen trained in Stanisław August's reign died off they were not replaced.

As for the magnates, some like the Radziwiłłs had connections at both the Russian and Prussian courts and led their lives principally in Saint Petersburg or Berlin. In late-nineteenth-century Galicia some aristocrats chose to make political careers in Vienna; indeed members of the Potocki, Gołuchowski, and Badeni families rose to be prime ministers. Both magnates and *szlachta* retained their estates unless forfeited for rebellion or lost through economic disaster—after the rising of 1830–31, for instance, some patriotic magnates had their estates confiscated. But the incentive to build or even rebuild on the grand scale was lacking, although there were naturally exceptions—minor alterations as at Rogalin, or an occasional major remodeling as at Gołuchów. Such building as there was, mainly urban, consciously harked back to the past, even searching for models in the remote villages of the Tatra Mountains (the so-called Zakopane style). Later, in fairness, some of the period's new styles were employed—Kraków, but not Warsaw, has a little good art-nouveau architecture. But Warsaw's Royal Castle, symbol of the country's heritage, was neglected by the Russians, who installed civil and military offices and removed part of its collections.

Instead Polish cultural talents were channeled into other fields such as literature, music, or painting. The diaspora produced some outstanding figures, who rejected eighteenth-century rationalism, yearned for free expression, and longed for an earlier idealized Poland. Adam Mickiewicz, a cosmopolitan and brilliant linguist, translator, and classicist, the friend of Pushkin, wrote great poetry in Paris, culminating in *Pan Tadeusz* (1834); Juliusz Słowacki was the nationalist movement's bard, producing beautiful lyric poetry; Zygmunt Krasiński's play *Undivine Comedy* was a masterpiece. Later in the nineteenth century poets were increasingly replaced by novelists as the nation's spokesmen, cool positivist analysts like Bolesław Prus. In music the immortal genius of Fryderyk Chopin was succeeded by fine composers like Henryk Wieniawski and Karol Szymanowski who, unlike Chopin, did not languish in exile. History painting as practiced by Jan Matejko evoked the myths of a heroic past, providing some panacea for the dreariness of foreign occupation. Fortunately by the early twentieth century representatives of other more modern styles such as Impressionism, the Viennese Secession, and even symbolism had established their reputations, evidence of Poland's determination to stay within the mainstream of European culture rather than wallow in indulgent nostalgia.

In 1918 the Poles could certainly not afford to wallow, for they faced enormous problems. Piłsudski, offspring of the Lithuanian *szlachta*, dreamed of reconstituting the Jagellonian commonwealth of Poland, Lithuania, and the Ukraine, while Dmowski demanded the pre-partition frontiers plus Upper Silesia and and East Prussia as a bulwark against Germany. The Allies, however, wished to set up a relatively small Polish state in which the Poles constituted a majority. This they did, giving it a minute Baltic coastline and making ethnically German Gdańsk a free city. An accord with Bolshevik Russia could only be reached by force of arms, but Piłsudski's invasion rebounded and by August 1920 the Soviet armies stood at the gates of Warsaw. In the so-called "eighteenth decisive battle of the world," Piłsudski routed them with a flank attack and peace was finally signed the next year.

The independent Poland's new constitution was modeled on that of the French Third Republic and its inherent defects led to weak governments that lasted on average five months. So Piłsudski, who had retired from politics, reemerged in 1926, mounted a coup d'état, and ruled as quasi-dictator until his death nine years later. Despite his immense achievements, he had destroyed parliamentary democracy without providing a substitute, and his successors were men of lesser stature. Their foreign policy was ill-conceived, for while they failed to create an alliance of Central European states they did encourage Nazi aggression against the former Czechoslovakia, seemingly without realizing they might become victims of it themselves.

During these interwar years, Polish architecture generally lacked distinction. The official style could be described as functional-classical, or more rudely Piłsudski populist—indeed it bore some resemblance to contemporary fascist buildings. At least Warsaw's Royal Castle, which became the official residence of the president of the republic, was properly restored and all its collections reunited under one roof. Innovative designs in the 1920s produced such projects as a garden city in the Żolibórz suburb of Warsaw and a few pleasant villas. The Brukalski and Syrkus families, for instance, commissioned schemes from such inventive architects as Romuald Gutt. Yet although life in most country houses continued uninterrupted by political convulsions, no more were built. With Warsaw a capital city once more, cultural and social life there revived, attracting both intellectuals and aristocrats—those from Galicia who had previously gathered in Kraków or Lwów, and others from Wielkopolska who had never regarded Poznań as a real cultural center.

The nobility's town palaces were opened up in early winter after the end of the shooting season. Although they were usually better furnished than their country seats, they were no longer run along prewar lines. In a difficult economic climate many estates were encumbered with debts, up to twice their notional value in some cases. Thus the Zamoyskis were forced to sell off a third of their property to right the family finances, requiring a special act of Parliament because with a "majorat" or entail it was forbidden to sell or mortgage land. The crash of 1929 disastrously affected some indebted landowners when the banks foreclosed on them. Additionally there were worries over land reform, which beginning in 1925 annually redistributed some two hundred thousand hectares, mainly from the larger estates. Landowners' protests on the subject were ignored, for their voice was not among the truly influential in the new Poland— even if Zamoyskis, Sapiehas, and Potockis held important political and diplomatic posts and much of the officer class was drawn from the ranks of the *szlachta*. Big estates survived nevertheless, especially in the eastern provinces. At Nieśwież the Radziwiłłs still possessed 104,000 hectares, although half of it was unproductive. And countless smaller properties existed, averaging around one thousand hectares with their dwory or small manor houses, of which there were reckoned to be over twenty thousand throughout the country in 1939 and around six hundred a decade later.

Count Maurice Zamoyski with his sisters in front of Klemensów, c. 1910. (Count Jan Zamoyski.)

Prince Stanisław Lubomirski in Polish national dress, 1920s. (Prince Stanisław Lubomirski.)

Few if any nations suffered catastrophe on the scale of the Poles in World War II. Once the Germans had invaded in September 1939, to be followed soon afterwards by the Russians in unholy alliance, economically and militarily weak Poland never stood a chance. All resistance ceased within a month and the victors divided the spoils. Germany annexed some provinces outright and ruled the rest from Kraków. In both zones of occupation Poles were deported *en masse* for slave labor or because they were viewed as social undesirables, and the Nazis began their systematic extermination of the sizeable Jewish community. A Polish government-in-exile was duly formed in London. By 1945 nearly 250 thousand Polish soldiers were fighting under British command and a further 400 thousand were active in the resistance known as the Home Army, which undertook extensive sabotage operations. As the Soviet forces pushed back the Germans, Warsaw rose against its occupiers in August 1944. But while the Russians sat on the opposite bank of the Vistula, the Wehrmacht totally destroyed the city, which had held out for two months. Stalin then proceeded to occupy the whole of ruined Poland, his theoretical ally, installing his handpicked Communist administration and excluding the government in London. At Yalta he gained agreement to redraw the Polish frontiers so that nearly half of the prewar state, including the two historic centers of Wilno and Lwów, was swallowed by Russia. In return it gave up half of East Prussia and territories up to the Oder-Neisse line containing seven million ethnic Germans. By ruthless manipulation of the political system, the Communists gained power in the "free" general election of 1947; thereafter the Sovietization of Poland began, turning it rapidly into a Russian satellite.

Amid all this devastation, a substantial part of the nation's cultural heritage had been destroyed. Warsaw had been obliterated, its Royal Castle razed on Hitler's express orders, and almost every town and city had been extensively damaged except Kraków, which miraculously emerged virtually unscathed. The Polish castles and country houses had undergone a similar fate: shelled, burned, and looted, the majority of their contents vanished. Yet forty-five years later most have arisen, like Warsaw and its Royal Castle, lovingly reconstructed stone by stone like a phoenix from the ashes. The fate of their former owners has been less fortunate. Every property over fifty hectares, and many under, were expropriated after the war, the buildings and contents included. In the conditions then prevailing, few were prepared to question the legality of this. Although in the postwar world their owners were regarded as members of an outcast, parasitic class, the vast majority chose to go on living in very reduced circumstances in their native country, perhaps feeling that their roots were of more importance than their comforts.

Polish history over the last millennium has been as dramatic, tragic, and intermittently uplifting as that of any European nation. Its triumphs and its all-too-frequent failures encapsulate the achievements and the shortcomings of humanity. But while only a handful of the monuments left deserve to rank among the architectural masterpieces of the continent, it would indeed take a foolish man to ignore the merits of Poland's castles and country houses, for they form an integral part of the cultural legacy of a remarkable people.

PIESKOWA SKAŁA

*I*t would be a misconception to characterize the Polish countryside as flat and featureless, for there are occasional enchanting surprises. One such may be found a mere twelve miles or so northwest of Kraków, off one of the main roads leading toward the great pilgrimage center of Częstochowa. There lies the Ojców valley, thickly wooded with steep cliffs and so full of geological curiosities as to merit that overworked word "picturesque." A favorite spot for eighteenth- and nineteenth-century artists as it is for countless tourists today, the valley also contains one of the grandest and best-preserved of Poland's medieval castles: Pieskowa Skała.

Little mention is made of the structure in early chronicles, although a document of 1315 from the reign of King Władysław I "the Short" (the monarch who reunited the country) refers to a modest wooden castle housing the royal garrison, which guarded the vital trade route from Kraków to Silesia. In his *Liber Beneficiorum* the fifteenth-century historian Jan Długosz, a cleric and tutor to the royal family, recorded that in the mid-fourteenth century Kazimierz the Great had erected a stone castle on the site, a high rocky bluff standing 120 feet above the Prądnik River. But its days as a royal fortress soon came to an end, for in 1377 Pieskowa Skała was presented to Piotr Szafraniec of Łuczyce in Małopolska, high steward of Kraków, in whose family's hands it was to remain for the next two centuries and more. Like many aristocratic families around this time, the Szafraniecs became rich by using their capital and influence at court to gain entry into various business enterprises, especially mining. Although the crown owned all mineral concessions, fortunes could certainly be made by developing the most lucrative of those deposits, including gold, as well as by closely supervising the mines and by keeping them drained and aerated. Thanks to its members' financial acumen the family was to retain its wealth, producing a string of notable courtiers and patrons of the Jagellon University (previously the Kraków University), one of whom, Jan, became rector in the 1420s; later on the Szafraniecs counted humanists and Protestant converts among their ranks.

During the fifteenth century the Szafraniecs transformed Pieskowa Skała into a castle with suitable grandeur. The original fortress had been built along a rock that occupied the northern edge of the site, but its outlines have been concealed by subsequent reconstruction. It was divided into an upper and a lower castle, joined and protected by curtain walls, although the disparity of height between the two parts of the castle was not considerable. The original Gothic architecture has now been largely obscured by subsequent reconstruction, but vestiges of it remain in the round tower with a ground-floor passage leading to it hewn out of the limestone rock of the northern range, or in the circular interior of the gateway to the courtyard, which shows the shape of the earlier gate-tower. A

Pieskowa Skała seen from the Ojców Valley, southern Poland near Kraków.

wall oven and a late-Gothic portal from this period also still exist, and many fragments of fifteenth-century walls stand, for the most part only reaching to the second floor.

A more fundamental reconstruction was undertaken in the sixteenth century. The Szafraniecs had remained a wealthy and important family: one of them, Hieronim, starosta or sheriff of Chęciny, had been one of the principal commanders during the 1530s in the army of Hetman Jan Amor Tarnowski, the founder of Polish military tactics; another, Stanisław, was a leading Protestant intellectual and humanist and founded a house of prayer for the Arians, an extreme sect otherwise known as the Socinians, who rejected the Trinity and the divine nature of Christ. Stanisław's tomb still lies in the castle chapel, and it was he who decided to remodel Pieskowa Skała in Renaissance style, work that was completed in 1578, according to an inscription over the gateway. The building's fundamental character was changed from that of functional fortress to magnate's residence. The main part of the lower castle was rebuilt around a rectangular courtyard lined by two-story arcaded galleries off of which led light spacious rooms. A slim loggia on two stories was built out next to the gate tower to afford views of the surrounding landscape. Attics crowned the roofs and rich sculptural decoration of realistically rendered human masks appeared on portals, window frames, fireplaces, and arcades. The splendid architecture was matched by the terraces, ponds, and gardens around the foot of the castle rock. Comparisons with the Wawel in nearby Kraków, so recently reconstructed and beautified by the Jagellon kings, were inescapable.

Early in the seventeenth century following Stanisław's death the Szafraniec family became extinct. Pieskowa Skała was then bought by another great noble dynasty from Małopolska, the Zebrzydowskis, who had already produced Andrzej, the redoubtable bishop of Kraków. The head of the family was the Palatine Mikołaj, a comrade-in-arms of Jan Zamoyski, and a man of many good works especially noted for his endowment of hospices and hospitals. Between 1605 and 1609 he also created only a short distance south of Kraków Poland's first Kalwaria, or Calvary, a popular place of pilgrimage. Here his Dutch architect, Paul Baudarth, laid out an open-air Way of the Cross along a hillside, with each of the fourteen stations possessing a chapel in a different style. Mikołaj had already sent a secretary to the Holy Land to establish the layout of all places relating to the Stations of the Cross and to measure the exact distances between them.

Not all of Zebrzydowski's actions were of an equally charitable nature.

He was the moving spirit in 1605 behind the convocation of a rival seym at Sandomierz, which voted to dethrone the Vasa king, Zygmunt III, for allowing his Jesuit advisers to propose abolishing established religious toleration. Mikołaj was no intellectual, but he personified the antiabsolutist and anticlerical discontent of many of the *szlachta*. Together with the other leaders of the bloodlessly suppressed abortive revolt, he was not penalized, and led a quiet life until his death in 1620. His son Michał also rose to high public office, becoming palatine of Kraków in his turn. He fortified Pieskowa Skała in the fashionable Italian style, endowing it with high bastions and a new entrance gate some way to the east, and enclosing the big outer forecourt within curtain walls. The castle chapel was refurbished and dedicated to his patron saint, Saint Michael, while the galleries around the courtyard were remodeled. Nevertheless none of this saved the castle from being sacked by Swedish troops in the course of their devastating invasion of 1655. For the remaining twelve years of his life, Michał was the proprietor of a semi-ruin, and after his death Pieskowa Skała was sold once more.

The new owners, the Wielopolskis, were also an ancient family from the region around Kraków, who traced their origins back to the eleventh century and had close blood ties to the fabulously rich Ossolińskis. Jan Wielopolski was a confidante of King Jan Kazimierz, who sent him to beg for the Habsburg emperor's help against the Swedes in 1656. Starosta and

later palatine of Kraków, he was then created count of Pieskowa Skała by the grateful sovereign. He restored the damaged buildings in baroque taste, walling in the open galleries and loggia while giving the outside elevations geometrical painted decoration. The interiors were furnished according to the latest fashions—during the eighteenth century this meant rooms with Dutch, Turkish, and Chinoiserie decor—and these interiors, together with the Wielopolskis' celebrated collections of treasures, earned for the castle the epithet "The Museum of Poland." Jan was married three times, the last time to the French-born Marie Anne d'Arquien de la Grange, sister of Jan Sobieski's queen. Daughter of a commander of a guards regiment at the French court who later became a cardinal, she had arrived to visit Poland in 1675 after her brother-in-law's election to the throne and had wed Wielopolski soon afterwards.

The family continued to prosper in the eighteenth century as father succeeded son for five generations. The Wielopolskis founded convents, made advantageous marriages, and played an intermittent role in national politics, several times as palatines of Kraków. In mid-century they inherited the rich entail and estate of Pińczów and assumed the additional surname of Myszkowski. But they made few changes at Pieskowa Skała, although it remained the principal of the family's several residences.

After the Napoleonic Wars Jan Wielopolski, the third Jan in the family line, was appointed a senator in the Congress Kingdom set up by the Russians and his title of count was officially recognized by the tsar. A tireless campaigner for justice and legal reform, he was also keen to promote his

Portrait of Maria Anna Wielopolska (née d'Arquien de la Grange) by Claude Callot, late seventeenth century.

Arcades in the courtyard.

country's industrial regeneration and established iron foundries with his own capital. His son Aleksander was equally remarkable, an intelligent, urbane aristocrat devoid of the romantic delusions so common among his contemporaries. He was sent to London in 1831 by the insurgent government to negotiate loans; there he realized the severe practical limits of the western powers' willingness to help the Poles, and he subsequently determined to find an accommodation with the Russian occupying power. Immensely capable, in particular with figures and statistics, Aleksander was placed in charge of the finances at Warsaw in the 1850s and propounded limited administrative, educational, and land-tenure reforms in return for the maintenance of order and the curbing of nationalist agitation. Unfortunately his scheme for selective conscription into the Russian army provided the direct spark for the insurrection of 1863 by excluding landowners and settled peasants and so ensuring that the burden fell principally on discontented town-dwellers and intellectuals. The result was only further repression, the shelving of his ideas, and the end to the political career of an unlucky yet courageous and patriotic man.

General view of the library.

Corner turret in the lower garden.

Not surprisingly the Wielopolskis, so engrossed in affairs of state in Warsaw, had begun to spend increasingly less time at Pieskowa Skała, which then lay in the Austrian-occupied part of Poland anyway. In 1842 the decision was taken to sell the property and it was bought by the Mieroszewski family. Unfortunately eight years later a severe fire destroyed the library plus many other interiors; the oldest buildings were also severely damaged and had to be demolished. Sobiesław Mieroszewski promptly began reconstruction, although it was still unfinished at the outbreak of the rising of 1863. On March 14 of that year Russian troops shelled and seized the burning castle, although a group of insurgents put up a stout defence. The next day Russians and Poles fought a stubborn battle at the village of Skała, just down the Ojców valley, from which the latter ultimately emerged victorious.

Undaunted by the disaster of the war, the Mieroszewskis started once more to restore Pieskowa Skała between 1864 and 1887. Although the money was lacking to return the interiors to their previous splendor, parts of the castle were again given a Gothic or rather neo-Gothic appearance, with small towers or turrets added here and there. The formal Italianate parterre was recreated, having originally been laid out in place of the former stables and coach house along the southern boundary of the forecourt and at a level some feet lower. Yet the expense proved too great for the family, which did not enjoy resources similar to their predecessors, the Wielopolskis, and in 1902 the whole property was put up for auction.

At first no prospective purchaser came forward and the future looked grim. But at the prospect of losing Pieskowa Skała an outcry ensued. By the twentieth century its status as a national monument had been assured, for almost all other medieval fortresses were in a state of total ruin; its magnificent setting and striking landscape had also been frequently mentioned in nineteenth-century literature and memoirs, even in the correspondence of Fryderyk Chopin. In response to the prospect of its loss a group of benefactors formed a joint-stock company called "The Castle of Pieskowa Skała," based in Warsaw. They raised the required price and converted the complex into a guesthouse. As such it survived both world wars, albeit in increasingly poor condition, until in 1950 Poland's State Monuments Commission undertook a thorough restoration.

Today Pieskowa Skała is again a remarkable castle, part medieval and part Renaissance. Under the aegis of the Wawel Museum administration it has acquired a variety of exhibits arranged in twelve rooms on the second and third floors. Additionally a collection of English pictures is housed together with the library from the Sapiehas family seat at Krasiczyn. In the most recent restoration, completed in 1963, the walled-in galleries and loggia were again uncovered, beamed ceilings were put back in the rooms, and stone door and window frames were reinstated.

For all its charm, the long-unlived-in castle lacks the personal warmth of a private home. Yet Pieskowa Skała should not be overlooked for that reason. Gaunt and austere as it appears, standing high above its river and silhouetted against the sky, its fine architecture is the product of three great Polish magnate families who lived there in succession, and their work has made it a national monument. In its many vicissitudes of fortune, in its periods of prosperity and of decay, Pieskowa Skała mirrors the history of its native land.

ŁAŃCUT

The notion that Poland is the gateway to Russia, even to the vast, empty steppes of Central Asia, becomes more vivid traveling east along the main road from Kraków. The landscape, although undulating, becomes barer and the towns, with their modern boxlike buildings, more charmless. But there are unexpected compensations. On the way to the border fortress of Przemyśl and the historic Polish city of Lwów, now incorporated into the Soviet Union, the large dusty village of Łańcut lies off a sharp bend of the road. In the middle of it, surrounded by extensive grounds and largely hidden from the world by discreet park railings, stands one of the grandest of Poland's country houses, more akin to a royal palace than a private residence.

A settlement has existed at Łańcut for over 650 years, as we know from that indefatigable chronicler Jan Długosz, later bishop of Lwów, who mentioned a property here in 1333 given by King Kazimierz the Great to his cousin Princess Elżbieta. It later passed to the family of Otto Pilecki, who built a wooden castle on a gentle slope, of which few traces remain. The Pileckis were of importance in the kingdom: Otto was a palatine and a close confidante of the king, while his wife, Jadwiga, stood sponsor to the pagan grand duke of Lithuania, Jagiełło, when he was Christianized and christened Władysław in the Wawel in 1386. The duke became a good friend of the Pileckis, frequently visiting Łańcut, and in 1417 as a long-time widower he secretly married their daughter Elżbieta, a move strongly opposed by his courtiers.

Although the castle of Łańcut remained in the hands of the Pileckis, little was done to it for the next two centuries. In 1580 it became the property of Stanisław Stadnicki, starosta or sheriff of Zygwold, whose hot temper and violent unruly behavior earned him the title of "the Łańcut Devil"—indeed it is still claimed that his ghost haunts the house. Between 1610 and 1620, Stadnicki's three sons constructed a new castle on the site. Its three wings formed a horseshoe-shaped courtyard facing south, their corners reinforced by projecting pentagonal turrets that marked a transition from the medieval fortress to a defence system based on outer bastions. The Stadnickis' tenure was short-lived, however, for two of the brothers were killed and in 1629 the third sold it to Stanisław Lubomirski.

As palatine of Kraków and a prince of the Holy Roman Empire, the new proprietor's talents as soldier and statesman were already established. Since 1615 the architect Matteo Trapola had been laboring to make the castle of Nowy Wiśnicz, one of his several enormous estates, into a worthy residence; now a similar transformation was to be undertaken at Łańcut. Until his death in 1637, Trapola was the man chiefly responsible for supervising the expansion and renovation of Łańcut. Lubomirski wanted it as thoroughly fortified as possible, according to the concepts expounded in the *Architectura Militaris* of Adam Freytag, a leading military theoretician of the time. Five bastions connected by curtain walls formed a pentagonal star, while the raised ramparts were provided with earthworks on which eighty cannon were placed. A deep dry moat enclosed in turn by another rampart surrounded the whole edifice. In the middle of

Garden facade of Łańcut, southeastern Poland.

Old view of the palace by Thomas de Thomon, late eighteenth century.

The sculpture gallery, with walls painted by Vincenzo Brenna in the late eighteenth century.

these fortifications the rectangular castle had been reoriented from a north–south to an east–west axis. Henceforth the entrance would be from the west, the village side, over a drawbridge across the moat and through a massive gateway; the village, also encircled by walls, would be connected to the castle too, an important strategic consideration.

Although the exterior was austere, for the elevations lacked any architectural features except for the baroque portal in the middle of the front facade, the interiors were sumptuous if not indeed palatial. Extra rooms had been gained by converting the corner turrets into habitable towers and replacing the loopholes with windows. From 1633 the royal stuccodor, Giovanni Battista Falconi, worked at Łańcut with his assistants. The dome of the Zodiac Room on the first floor of the northwestern tower, so-called because the signs of the zodiac were painted on the ceiling, was certainly decorated by him; there, lavish baroque stucco work surrounded the painted allegories symbolizing the four seasons of the year. Falconi was also responsible for the ceiling of a room called the Great Antechamber as well as other interiors since destroyed. Major work at Łańcut lasted twelve years until 1641, although polychromed beams dated 1642 have recently been uncovered.

Stanisław died in 1649 and was succeeded by his son Jerzy Sebastian, who, as marshal of the crown and field hetman, occupied half the great offices of the Polish state. He loyally supported King Jan Kazimierz, and it was at Łańcut that representatives of the Polish nobility signed a pact binding them to repel the invading Swedes. Nevertheless the latter's ally György Rákóczi captured the area with his Transylvanian army in 1657 and burned the village, although fortunately the castle was spared. Jerzy was one of the most energetic Polish generals, but he suffered badly in the war when the Swedes pillaged his seat at Nowy Wiśnicz, carrying off 152 wagonloads of plunder. In retaliation he led a daring raid into Transylvania, forcing Rákóczi's troops to withdraw precipitately. Łańcut was not left in good repair, of course, so when Stanisław Herakliusz Lubomirski took over from his father, he decided to have it restored by his protégé, the architect Tylman van Gameren. The need became more imperative after a bad fire in 1688, but since the plans have been lost it is impossible to know all that Tylman did. He certainly remodeled the towers in late baroque taste, modernized the fortifications, repositioned various windows, widened the main staircase, and divided the Great Antechamber into an entrance hall and another smaller room.

The last of the Lubomirskis to own Łańcut, another Stanisław, inherited it as a young man in 1745. Eight years thereafter he was to marry Izabela Czartoryska, an energetic, highly educated, and immensely rich figure in her own right who had once been considered as a possible bride for her cousin King Stanisław August. Under their aegis Łańcut was transformed from a heavily fortified castle of an essentially severe character into a true palace, a worthy residence for the grandest magnate. Work started in the 1770s and, despite Stanisław's death in 1783, continued with short intervals until Izabela herself died at the age of eighty in 1816.

On the north and east fronts, all twin windows were eliminated and regularly spaced replacements were put in. The castle itself was extended by elongating the west wing at its southern end, so creating the Great Dining Room, as it was called, and a pavilion was added behind the northwestern tower to house the library. Most of the ramparts were leveled and a landscape park with neoclassical buildings was laid out by degrees. Initially the family's architect, Hieronim Jędrzejowski, was used, but some of the most distinguished exponents of neoclassicism in Poland were later employed too.

The decoration of the interiors began in earnest in the 1780s. Vincenzo Brenna, a Florentine painter who subsequently worked at Pavlovsk for Tsar Paul, produced a variety of antique, arabesque, and grotesque painted motifs, which adorned the walls of what was known as the Chinese Chamber on the second floor and a guest apartment with a study and bedroom on the ground floor. In the Views Room his work was supplemented

The Hall of Columns with Antonio Canova's
statue of Izabela Lubomirska's adopted son Henryk
as Cupid.

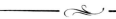

The court theatre at Łańcut, inaugurated in 1792.

Lions forming the base of a fountain in the garden.

by two oval murals depicting Łańcut, while in the sculpture gallery he created the illusion of an ancient sunlit ruin overgrown with vines. Other artists were commissioned as well—many of the doors, for instance, were decorated from drawings done by Franciszek Smuglewicz. The magnificent rococo paneling in the Mirrored Study, with wonderfully delicate gilt frames, was probably imported from South Germany.

Szymon Bogumił Zug, who had already worked for Izabela at Natolin and Wilanów, and had helped her design the landscape park at Mokotów, was soon brought to Łańcut and was joined in 1796 by his collaborator Jan Chrystian Kamsetzer. Together they designed Izabela's bedroom and the adjoining salon in Louis XIV style, along with the Hall of Columns at one end of the sculpture gallery, where a circle of Ionic pillars framed a statue from 1787 by Antonio Canova depicting the princess's adopted son, Henryk Lubomirski, as Cupid. Yet it was Chrystian Piotr Aigner, imported during the 1790s, who made the most significant contribution. In company with his accomplished stuccodor Fryderyk Bauman, he created the interiors of the state rooms in the west wing: the vast ballroom, the Great Dining Room, the theatre, and the chapel. In the first two the arrangement of the wall panels was carefully and logically planned and the restrained decoration was harmonized with the architecture. Equally elegant were the small chapel in the southwestern tower of the west wing, with its coffered, rose-encrusted dome, and the lovely theatre, which could seat an audience of ninety in its stalls and gallery.

Izabela greatly enjoyed entertaining in a style suitable to the grand palace she had brought into being. Music and drama flourished at Łańcut as she hired a court composer, Marcello di Capua, and a Haydn pupil named Peter Hänsel as kapellmeister. The princess herself played the clavichord in the palace's small orchestra, and commissioned numerous musical pieces, mainly operatic, which have been preserved in the archives. In 1792 the theatre was inaugurated with a performance of *Parady*, five humorous one-act plays written by her son-in-law Jan Potocki. In her widowhood, Izabela traveled all over Europe, bringing back most of Łańcut's antique sculpture collection from a buying trip to Rome in 1786. She purchased paintings and furniture extensively in Paris, too, where she became a close friend of Queen Marie Antoinette. Loathing the French Revolution and its Napoleonic aftermath, she welcomed to Łańcut such Bourbon princes as the future kings Louis XVIII and Charles X as well as their sister Queen Maria Carolina of Naples and Madame Anne Louise Germaine de Stäel.

Despite her eighteen other residences, the princess regularly visited Łańcut, which was kept fully staffed with around two hundred servants, inside and out. Improvements continued after 1800 as Aigner remodelled the main facade and, in association with Bauman, designed a variety of buildings for the gardens. Chief among these was the well-proportioned neoclassical orangery finished in 1802, its roof concealed by an attic and an Ionic-columned portico under a triangular pediment. Several years later a neoclassical house by the northern gates to the park, which had originally been erected by Kamsetzer's pupil Jan Griesmeyer, was rebuilt by Aigner into a little romantic castle in a neo-Gothic style, with Bauman's stucco work inside; there the family could escape from the formal life of the palace. In 1810 the pair constructed a gloriette, or folly, in the form of a semicircular Corinthian colonnade on the northwest bastion. Inside redecoration went on. The walls of the Chinese Chamber and the adjacent parlor, decorated in Pompeian taste, were covered by tiny, brightly-colored textile fragments glued to a linen base to simulate oriental wallpaper, although they concealed Brenna's painting.

When Izabela Lubomirska died in 1816, her enormous estates were divided among her heirs. Łańcut was inherited by her grandson Alfred Potocki, whose mother, Julia, had died over twenty years before. His father, Jan, a genuine polymath (writer, archaeologist, and traveler), had never cared to share the house with its redoubtable owner, preferring instead to live on his own property of Uładówka in Podolia. There the previous year, in a fit of depression over the treatment of Polish aspirations at the Congress of Vienna, he had committed suicide. Alfred was a good patriot too as well as a Francophile, and with his brother he fought under Marshal Józef Poniatowski in Napoleon's Russian campaign of 1812. Held prisoner for two years, he then returned and married his cousin Józefina Czartoryska. Yet compared with his father he was no fiery nationalist, choosing instead to stay on good terms with the Austrian government and opposing the several rebellions in Galicia against its rule. He also took advantage of the Austrian legal structure in 1821 to turn Łańcut into an entail, requiring that the huge property be passed down intact—although part of Izabela's collections had already been left to her adopted son, Henryk Lubomirski, who lived at neighboring Przeworsk.

Alfred also continued to improve Łańcut by removing the remaining interior ramparts, leveling the ground in front of the palace, and demolishing the entrance gates and drawbridge. These were replaced by a neo-Gothic gateway and a railed stone bridge across the moat. Various small buildings in the park were renovated—a hermitage, an Orthodox church, and a cottage orné (all now vanished)—while a neoclassical *manège* or riding school was constructed in 1828–30 to the plans of Ludwik Bogochwalski. A landscape architect, Jan Zulauf, was put in charge of the gardens, and greenhouses for oranges and peaches were erected. Aigner and Bauman, who still paid intermittent visits to Łańcut, were involved with the partial Gothicization of the north and east facades. And during the 1830s fine parquet floors, locally made to designs by Karol Chodziński, were laid in various rooms in the palace.

At his death in 1862, Alfred was succeeded by his son. Unlike his father, Alfred II pursued an active political career, mainly at Vienna where

The ballroom designed by Chrystian Piotr Aigner, c. 1800.

he became minister of agriculture, briefly prime minister, and a close confidante of Emperor Francis Joseph. But he also served for eight years as governor of Galicia, and helped found the Academy of Kraków. His wife, Maria, was the daughter of Prince Roman Sanguszko, who had walked to Siberia in chains after the Poles rose against their Russian masters in 1830, and became the eponymous hero of Joseph Conrad's short story. She also brought an immense dowry with her to add to the Potockis' possessions. But with so busy a public life her husband had little time to visit Łańcut, where no new projects were undertaken, inside or out, and which suffered from a lack of maintenance.

Their elder son, Roman, inherited Łańcut in 1889 and for the next two-and-a-half decades was responsible for the third major reconstruction of the palace. In this he was ably assisted by his second wife, Elżbieta Radziwiłł, known as "Betka." Two architects, Armand Bauqué and Alberto Pio, were employed with a variety of craftsmen from Paris and Vienna. They extended the library pavilion at one end of the west wing and built out the Great Dining Room so that it could now seat over a hundred guests. A short south wing was added just near the dining room, thus forming a second small courtyard. Roman and Betka also began to modernize Łańcut, installing a new water supply through sixteen miles of piping as well as sewerage, central heating, electricity, and even telephones. The best interiors were retained but many others were redecorated in historicizing nineteenth-century style. At the neglected theatre, refurbished by the Austrian architects Hermann Helmer and Ferdinand Fellner, performances recommenced and new scenery changes were made.

Exterior changes were equally extensive, and during these years the landscape park assumed its present shape. Within the area enclosed by the dry moat a seventeenth-century powder magazine was demolished, an Italian parterre laid out in front of the eastern wing, and a rose garden created to the south of the orangery, all under the aegis of a gardener called Maxwald, who had formerly worked for the Rothschilds. The English garden was also reestablished and a diversity of flowers cultivated, especially orchids, pinks, and roses. Bauqué built a large complex of stables and a coach house, for Roman loved horses and carriages and collected the variety of equipages that form the nucleus of the exhibition now on display at Łańcut. Lastly all the facades of the palace were again remodeled in French neobaroque style, although the distinctive twin onion domes flanking the entrance front were kept.

With the outbreak of World War I, Galicia was on the frontline of hostilities, although both tsar and kaiser instructed their commanders not to damage Łańcut. During six months in 1914–15 it changed hands four times between the Russian and the Austro–German armies. The Potockis returned in the summer of 1915 to find the palace virtually undamaged, although the farms and forests indeed suffered terribly. But Roman, whose health was weak anyway, died a few weeks later and was succeeded by his elder son, yet another Alfred. The end of the war brought a further host of problems. Polish independence and the Russian revolution meant that some of the Potockis' eastern properties, like Antoniny where Roman's younger brother had lived, were lost to the Soviet Union. The family's entire entailed esate amounted to some forty thousand acres, the income from which was insufficient to cover the vast upkeep costs at Łańcut. In fact the estate's non-entailed lands were larger and more productive, but the war had drastically reduced both the labor force and the family's revenue. The already-evident fact was that only industrial development rather than agriculture could support the Potockis' way of life, and between the wars Alfred sold land and invested with varying success in a variety of enterprises: banks, oil companies, distilleries, coal mines, or brickworks. Despite a fairly healthy financial situation, however, he found it necessary periodically to raise capital.

Portrait of Jan Potocki by Giovanni Battista Lampi, late eighteenth century.

Frieze of horses' heads on the riding school.

Carriages in the coach house.

Nevertheless life carried on at Łańcut with all the old splendor: a private orchestra still performed, hunting and shoots continued, and enormous house parties were held attended by European royalty, aristocrats, and members of cafe society. Entertaining was mostly done during August and September, intermittently in the winter shooting season, and again from late spring to early summer. Łańcut's huge staff ensured that everything ran smoothly, including the wooden shooting lodge a few miles away at Julin, the Arabian and thoroughbred stud at Albigowa, and the immaculate hunt kennels. As Alfred wrote in his memoirs: "Year by year the number of guests increased. . . . in entertaining them and keeping open Łańcut as a meeting place for diplomats and distinguished foreign visitors, I believed that I was serving my country." A golf course was built, Turkish baths were installed, and on a less significant level, minor alterations were made inside the palace. The collections were much enhanced in the 1920s, especially in the field of painting, by a magnificent bequest from Alfred's cousin Mikołaj Potocki.

In 1925 Łańcut was designated a national monument and major conservation work was scheduled for 1939 before World War II intervened. On the outbreak of war, the Polish army immediately requisitioned three-fifths of the estate's horses. But within a week German troops arrived, occupying the Orangery and the second floor of the palace—although they did not damage the palace. When Hitler and Stalin partitioned Poland, Łańcut remained in the German sphere, but the border ran not far away along the San River. Alfred was arrested and interrogated several times by the Gestapo, although never held for long. It appears, in fact, that he held aloof from all the Underground activities, despite his later claims of having assisted them. By early 1944 Alfred recognized that a Russian victory was inevitable, so before his own departure in July he organized the systematic packing of some six hundred cases containing the cream of the

Early twentieth-century bathroom in the tower.

Portrait of Betka Potocka (née Radziwiłł) by Czederowski, early twentieth century.

Meet of the Potocki hunt outside the stables at Antoniny, now in the Ukraine, pre-1914.

Alfred Potocki driving the Duke and Duchess of Kent, 1937.

palace's contents. With German cooperation they were sent to Vienna by train. After various problems they reached his cousins in Liechtenstein, and eventually he took them into exile in France. After his octogenarian mother's death, Alfred married a Polish-American, published his memoirs, and died childless in 1958. Tragically, his possessions never returned to Poland, for the Communist régime refused to negotiate with a man they insisted on regarding as a traitor.

Fortunately the Soviet army that reached Łańcut in August 1944 did not occupy the palace—indeed orders were issued for its protection. That November the palace was officially opened to the public as a museum, although repairs and conservation work continued throughout the 1950s. Today the buildings are in excellent condition, and possess a slightly less lifeless feel than is usually the case with the great houses in former Iron Curtain countries. Quite a large number of the palace's 308 rooms are open to visitors. Yet even if Łańcut appears well furnished, only a quarter of the paintings and a bare third of the sculpture originate from its prewar contents, just as the tapestry, furniture, plate, and porcelain collections have also been grievously depleted.

Despite the loss of much of its original furnishings, Łańcut ranks as one of the grandest private residences in Poland—indeed in all of Europe. Over the past four-and-a-half centuries its fate has been closely bound up with that of two of the greatest Polish magnate families, the Lubomirskis and the Potockis, and it has reflected their wealth and glory even as it has suffered in their tribulations. Any visitor to it will appreciate what a showcase of the nation's cultural and aesthetic achievements it affords, for Łańcut remains a palace of legendary splendor.

BARANÓW

*I*f a river can be said to embody the soul of a country, we can see Poland most clearly in the path of the Vistula, just as Czechoslovakia is revealed by the Vltava and Hungary by the Danube. In its long course from its source in the Tatra Mountains to its estuary emptying into the Baltic Sea near Gdańsk, the Vistula flows almost the whole length of the country through some of its most historic regions. Wending its way through the heart of Małopolska, a short distance upstream from the ancient town of Sandomierz it passes by Baranów, one of the finest of all Polish Renaissance castles.

According to Anton Schneider, a mid-nineteenth-century historian, a wooden fortress existed on the site of Baranów by the early twelfth century. Built by Bogusław Jaksyc, a lieutenant of King Bolesław the Wrymouth who later rose to be governor of Pomerania, the fort was established to control this stretch of the Vistula. Nearby an important ford crossed the river to the high left bank, along which ran the trade route from Kraków to Sandomierz. By the thirteenth century the fort had become the property of the Gozdawa family, who kept it in good condition and afforded the local inhabitants a degree of protection against the numerous Tatar invasions. Paweł, the last of the Gozdawas, supposedly entertained King Kazimierz the Great there before accompanying his sovereign on a campaign into Ruthenia where he was killed.

The king then presented Baranów to a knight of outstanding prowess known as Pietrasz, who had reputedly saved his royal master's life in the Ruthenian war. From him descended the Baranowski family, who took their name from Baranów. But both names derive from "Baran," which means ram in Polish, for this was great sheep-breeding country. Here cloth weaving flourished too, and the local guild of clothworkers remained active until the nineteenth century. Especially from 1500 onward the grain trade was of commercial importance; silos were constructed along the river banks to store grain brought from the interior before it was floated on barges down the Vistula to Gdańsk and later exported. Positioned between the Vistula and its tributary the Babulowka and surrounded by ponds and water meadows that regularly flooded, the virtually impregnable Baranów was well able to dominate and guard the surrounding countryside.

By the sixteenth century the castle had again changed hands, twice in fact, and was now owned by the Górka family from Wielkopolska. They extended and modernized the existing fortress, although it was still a building entirely designed for military purposes. In 1569 Stanisław Górka sold the property to Rafał Leszczyński, starosta or sheriff of Radziejów, member of a rising noble dynasty, and also a native of Wielkopolska. Rafał was notable both for his ability to make money and for his advocacy of the reform program advocated by the executionist movement. When presiding over the Seym he had continually called for a reorganization of the army, and for equal rights for religious dissenters; indeed he had a personal interest at stake, for he was a member of the Czech Brethren in Poland, also known as the Arians, a strict Calvinist sect for whom he

*Corner view of main facade at Baranów,
southeastern Poland.*

had built a college and church at Leszno and a chapel on his estate at Gołuchów.

Although he lived on until 1592, a mere ten years after his purchase of Baranów, Rafał passed on the property to his eldest son, Andrzej. The latter was a famous warrior who participated in all the wars waged by Poland in the mid-sixteenth century, but he was also a widely traveled patron of art and learning, who corresponded with scholars all over Europe. Realizing Baranów's favorable position for defence, commerce, and communications, he made it his principal residence and entertained King Stefan Báthory there on several occasions. But the cramped medieval fortress was not to his taste and within a few years he had decided to rebuild.

The architect he commissioned was perhaps the most famous then working in Poland. A native Florentine of about sixty who had spent almost two-thirds of his life in his adopted country, Santi Gucci had developed an idiosyncratic and capricious style of his own, which relied strongly on such decorative elements as Ionic volutes, concentric bosses, low wide bands of acanthus leaves, and flamboyant vases. His connections with the royal court, for which he had undertaken many projects, was very close, and he now had a large atelier to assist him. Although conclusive documentary proof that Gucci was the main architect is lacking, much of the work at Baranów—the richly decorated portals along the upper galleries, for example—can be closely linked on stylistic grounds to his funerary monuments in the Wawel's cathedral, to the Firlej family tombs at Janowiec, and to the castle of Mirów. Baranów was a happy symbiosis of Italian theory and Polish practice.

Work began at Baranów in 1591 and lasted until 1606—in the last few years under his pupils' supervision, for Gucci had died. The result was a rectangular building some eighty by forty-three yards in roughly a two-to-one ratio. The blocks appeared massive, but the quite slender round

Front door with sundial above it.

68

Entrance block of main facade.

Ceiling in the Tower Room, with plasterwork by Giovanni Battista Falconi, early seventeenth century.

towers at each of the four corners, with helmets underset on their longer sides by decorative gables, imposed a compositional discipline on the whole. An attic-crowned block containing the entrance gate projected from the center of the front facade, and attics were later added on to both of the sides.

With an interior courtyard surrounded by arcaded galleries, Baranów received a fairly traditional Renaissance layout, yet its design was highly polished. The front facade was formed merely of a curtain wall, which joined onto the remaining three wings on a rectangular ground plan. Gucci raised the level of the courtyard three meters to prevent any flooding from the Vistula, so internally the building had one less story than it appeared to from the outside. Closed by an iron gate, which had been given an artfully carved grille, the arched entrance doorway with square stone surrounds led up a flight of steps into the courtyard. Directly ahead a vaulted, two-branched staircase, facing out onto the courtyard and supported on the arcade, led to the upper level, its lower part open between arches resting on columns and joined by a balustrade. The arcaded galleries, rising through two stories, surrounded the other three sides of the courtyard, with the reception rooms and bedrooms leading off them. The gallery columns had Ionic capitals on both levels, although the lower ones rested on socles, the bases of which were decorated by grotesquely carved faces, or mascarons. The rosettes in the spandrels of the archivolts were equally typical features. Colored friezes, recently unveiled during restoration, adorned the outer facades and ran along the courtyard walls. The polychromatic heraldic devices simultaneously uncovered under the arcades and on the staircase's vaulted ceiling were from the same period.

The Leszczyńskis' new castle soon became a cultural center filled with numerous works of art and a notable library. Under the influence of Andrzej, a staunch Calvinist, the Baranów parish church ceased to be Catholic and a printing press was established in the village to disseminate the

Vaulted ceiling of the courtyard staircase.

The external staircase and arcades in the courtyard.

Row of grotesque heads in the courtyard.

works of famous Protestant theologians. Andrzej's death in 1606 coincided with the completion of the main reconstruction. His son Rafał, palatine of Bełz and another enlightened statesman, succeeded him and further added to the library. During the thirty years of his ownership further work was carried out on the attics of the two long facades—the front curtain wall and the back—and on the outer fortifications that surrounded the castle— the latter a typical attribute of a *palazzo in fortezza*. Today solely the underground foundations of these elements are visible, for the portions remaining aboveground were demolished during the nineteenth century to allow the erection of protecting walls along the Vistula escarpment.

Rafał was a great landowner with many other residences, although he spent much of his time at Baranów. Evidence of the scale on which he lived is provided by the fact that when his wife died in 1635 he supplied over two thousand mourning costumes for his servants, a number that excluded the kitchen staff, since they were never seen. This proved to be a sensible measure, for he himself followed her the next year. His successors were first his son, another Andrzej, and then his grandson Samuel, but the latter could no longer finance the accumulated debts on the estate and sold it to his paternal uncle, Bogusław, chancellor of the Kingdom. Only one more generation of Leszczyńskis was to live at Baranów, for Bogusław's son Rafał III, the royal treasurer and ambassador to Constantinople who played a notable part in lifting the Turkish siege of Vienna in 1683, sold the property in 1677. The Leszczyńskis did not fade away altogether after that—Rafał's son Stanisław was to be twice elected king of Poland, although he enjoyed a very short reign, was twice dethroned, and retired to France as duke of Lorraine, where he created one of Europe's most perfect eighteenth-century cities at Nancy. His daughter Marie would also become the faithful, long-suffering wife of the notoriously dissolute King Louis XV of France.

The purchaser of Baranów was Prince Dmitry Wiśniowiecki, scion of one of the great Ruthenian aristocratic houses. But he only survived for six more years, and after a brief interval his widow, Teofila, married Prince Karol Józef Lubomirski, a union of two major fortunes. By this date

The picture gallery built by Tylman van Gameren
in the late seventeenth century.

Portrait of Queen Marie of France, daughter of
Rafał Leszczyński, by Jean-Marc Nattier,
mid-eighteenth century.

Old view of Baranów by Napoleon Orda,
nineteenth century. (Łańcut collection.)

the Lubomirskis' estates stretched much of the way from Kraków to Lwów, and Baranów became just one of the family's many residences. However, substantial sums of money were available for the upkeep or renovation of the castle. From the Lubomirskis' point of view one drawback to Baranów was that none of the rooms were large enough to permit entertaining on a really grandiose scale. They decided to rectify that and accordingly commissioned Tylman van Gameren to refurbish the interiors. He introduced baroque plasterwork into many of the rooms, while in the west wing he created a long picture gallery with two adjoining antechambers to make an appropriate enfilade of rooms. The rich heavy stucco decoration is as magnificent now as in the late seventeenth century, but sadly the main feature, the specially carved frames with enormous canvases of landscape scenes that lined the new picture gallery, has been replaced by insipid modern copies.

Karol Józef Lubomirski's son and then his granddaughter inherited Baranów. In the course of the next seventy years it continued to change hands through sale or marriage several times, until in 1771 Józef Potocki bought it. His daughter Anna received the estate as her dowry when she wed Jan Krasicki and their descendants were to keep Baranów until the late nineteenth century, filling it with valuable contents, furniture, objets d'art, and a fine picture collection as well as building up the library once more with many precious books and manuscripts. There were also many mementoes of a cousin, Bishop Ignacy Krasicki; a true child of the Enlightenment, he was a poet, playwright, essayist, biographer, and author of a delightful book entitled *Fables*.

Tragically everything was lost in a terrible fire that broke out in September 1849 and devastated Baranów. After this catastrophe the Krasickis lacked both the money and the will to restore the castle to its former splendor. They also seemed to lack any interest in their few remaining art treasures, and no repairs were undertaken to make good the damage. At

length the property was put up for auction, and in 1867 it was bought by Feliks Dolański, who immediately set about the restoration. This proved an enormous task, but before it was finished another fire in 1898 set back the work again by several more years. Yet the Dolańskis—Feliks and his son Stanisław Karol—remained undaunted, ably supported by their supervising architect, Tadeusz Stryjeński from Kraków. One of the main rooms at courtyard level, for example, was successfully converted into a chapel, with fine art-nouveau stained-glass windows designed by Józef Mehoffer and an altar triptych by Jacek Malczewski.

During World War II the Dolańskis yet again experienced the sadness of seeing their work destroyed as the castle endured fierce fighting. In the autumn of 1944 the Russians crossed the Vistula near Baranów to establish a bridgehead, which held out against repeated German attacks until the big Soviet offensive begun in January 1945 swept the fighting westward. The castle was not obliterated by the shellfire, but did suffer extensive structural damage, while all the contents not previously removed were smashed or stolen. Nevertheless the Dolańskis continued to retain Baranów until it was expropriated in the wake of the Communist takeover in 1945.

Despite the castle's desperate condition, in 1956 the Ministry of Culture started a major restoration program and two years later its efforts were joined by the Ministry for Chemical Industry. The discovery of large sulfur deposits in the neighborhood had revolutionized Baranów's prospects, for a renovated castle could obviously be used as a center for conferences and for business entertaining. Executed at a very high standard, the work was supervised by Professor Alfred Majewski, whose team had been responsible for repairs to the Wawel. New exhibits were loaned by museums, and the rooms on the upper two stories again resembled castle interiors, albeit somewhat sparsely furnished; an archaeological and geographical exhibition concerning the sulfur industry was also arranged on the ground floor.

Baranów is not the best known or most accessible of Poland's surviving great houses. Yet in purer form than almost anywhere else it encapsulates the finest flowering of Renaissance architecture, unencumbered by the legacy of the Middle Ages, for only vestigial traces of the medieval fortress are still visible. Quite apart from its historical interest, which is compelling enough on its own merits, Baranów is one of Poland's most satisfying and beautiful monuments.

WILANÓW

Main facade of Wilanów, near Warsaw.

Monumental doorway in one of the side wings.

Many of the major cities of Europe have a great summer palace on their outskirts built during the seventeenth or eighteenth century: Versailles, Schönbrunn, Sans Souci, Nymphenburg, and Caserta, to name but a few. Warsaw is not lacking in this respect either, for on its southeastern edge and beyond the suburbs stands the palace of Wilanów. This magnificent baroque residence belonged to a succession of the nation's most remarkable families both royal and noble, and its history provides any visitor with a fascinating glimpse into the history of Poland itself.

In the mid-seventeenth century the first foundations of a building at the Wilanów estate were laid. Bogusław Leszczyński, the owner, planned a rectangular block with small alcove towers at the corners and two larger octagonal towers farther away linked to the main building by screen walls. Work had not progressed very far when the property was sold to King Jan Sobieski in 1677. Ever since his accession to the throne three years before, the king, essentially a countryman, had hankered for a rural retreat near the capital, for his own family residences were far away to the east and he found Warsaw's Royal Castle uncomfortable. At Wilanów he had discovered precisely what he wanted.

Since funds were limited, Sobieski instructed his court architect, Augustyn Locci, to utilize the existing foundations with various adjustments. Without delay work began in May 1677, and within two years the first phase in the building was completed. On the site of Leszczyński's center block a modest one-story manor house had been constructed under a high hipped roof with four corner alcoves, each with its own little roof. No wings or towers were constructed, but two outbuildings faced each other to form a small courtyard in the front. Behind, a modest garden containing several ponds gave an idyllic, rustic character to the place.

In 1681–82 a second phase of construction began that transformed Wilanów into a much grander residence. Both the main block and the alcoves were raised half a story, while open galleries instead of the screen walls Leszczyński had envisaged linked this structure to imposing square towers erected on the octagonal foundations. The galleries were given monumental portals shaped like triumphant Roman arches, and all the facades were covered with stucco sculpture executed by Italian and Polish craftsmen. The front elevation was divided by monumental pilasters supporting an elaborately sculpted pediment, which depicted a solar orb surrounded by allegorical figures of fame blowing trumpets; cherubs holding up the Sobieski coat of arms and a statue of Minerva crowned the whole. Balustraded attics also crowned the end towers, with stone statues of the Muses imported from Holland standing at each corner.

A final phase of building started in 1684 and continued intermittently until Sobieski's death in 1696. During these years an entire additional story was constructed over the central part of the main block, the sculptural decoration from the dismantled pediment was transferred to its facade, and the statues of the Muses were moved to adorn the roof line. The front elevations of the corner alcoves facing the courtyard were given an attic level covered with statues of ancient goddesses and with bas-reliefs glorifying Sobieski's military victories. The sculptor Stefan Szwaner from Gdańsk was responsible for these and for the compositions filling the archivolts of the galleries.

The grounds were also laid out by the royal engineer, Adolf Boy, in a style hitherto virtually unseen in Poland. The large courtyard in front of the palace—for this is what Wilanów had now become—was divided into two sections. The front area was framed by the coach house and storehouse and was entered through a handsome stone gateway crowned by martial trophies, while the rear part, surrounded by the principal buildings, was separated from the front by a low, ornamentally carved wall. Behind the palace a geometric Italian garden on two levels sloped down to the lake. The upper parterre contained box trees, stone urns, and mythological gilt figures cast in the Gdańsk bell foundry, as well as red marble fountains and wooden summerhouses with green and gilt roofs. A double flight of steps led down to the lower parterre, which contained two rectangular ponds. To one side of the garden the orchard was planted with a range of fruit trees behind the stables and granaries. The entire landscape was designed along a symmetrical central axis from the entrance gate through to the lake, beyond which a straight canal extended, prolonging the line. A vegetable garden and a farmyard situated to the south formed the only other deviations from this geometric layout.

The interior of Wilanów was equally symmetrical although by contrast to Italian custom the main rooms were situated on the ground floor and not on the piano nobile. The cavernous entrance hall rising through two stories led onto the drawing room behind and formed a definite axis dividing the king's apartments from the queen's. Each of their suites had a large antechamber leading directly off the hall and a bedchamber of similar proportions, along with several other smaller rooms. On the mezzanine floor the rooms had relatively low ceilings, but in the belvedere created by adding a level to the central part a magnificent banqueting hall was installed.

To decorate his new palace Sobieski set up an atelier, which was to grow into the first academy of painting in Poland. The French painters Claude Callot and Abraham Paris were joined by the Polish artists Jerzy Szymonowicz-Siemigonowski and Jan Reisner. A team of sculptors and stuccodores also collaborated with them, and many other skilled craftsmen were employed as well. The Italo-French influence was paramount:

Family group with King Jan Sobieski and Queen Marie-Casimire, c. 1693.

Old view of Wilanów by Bernardo Bellotto, 1776.
(Royal Castle of Warsaw.)

Central tower seen from the garden.

the royal bedchambers were modeled on Pietro da Cortona's designs for the Pitti Palace, for instance, while Szymonowicz-Siemigonowski's ceiling paintings owe much to Carlo Maratta and Nicholas Poussin. Yet the polychrome decoration of the ceiling beams was typically Polish, and Dutch taste was also apparent in the choice of some of the furniture and pictures. Much was intended to extol Sobieski's glory, like the enormous equestrian statue placed in the entrance hall of the king trampling down the Turks, or the self-aggrandizing portraits of himself and his family in a variety of poses. Yet his sincere interest in incorporating Poland's art into the classical European mainstream was unquestionable and the work he commissioned was often very fine.

By the end of the seventeenth century the modest manor house had been turned into an Italianate baroque palace. Locci had certainly looked to Rome for his inspiration, but he also cleverly adapted many motifs to match Polish styles and his master's Sarmatian tastes. If Sobieski had not died in 1696 perhaps Wilanów might almost have become a rival to Versailles, for the King's personal and dynastic ambitions were boundless as were those of his French queen, Marie-Casimire. Within days of his death, however, all valuables were moved to safekeeping in Warsaw, and the best furniture and pictures were locked away in the palace treasuries. Two of his three sons, Aleksander and Konstanty, inherited Wilanów. The former continued to extend the palace wings until, utterly disappointed in his hopes for the throne, he retired to Rome where he was ordained as a Capuchin monk. Now the sole owner, Konstanty took scant interest in the property, and his straitened financial circumstances precluded any further improvements. Largely emptied of their contents, the buildings began to decay. In 1720 Konstanty sold Wilanów to the daughter of Stanisław Herakliusz Lubomirski, Elżbieta Sieniawska, whose husband was both grand hetman and palatine of Kraków.

For the remainder of the eighteenth century Wilanów was owned by three rich, powerful, and determined women in succession, grandmother, mother and daughter. Elżbieta, the first, already possessed several other properties including Puławy. She was an art connoisseur with definite tastes who regularly bought German silver and porcelain along with fine fabrics, clocks, and chandeliers from a variety of dealers. Upon purchasing Wilanów she decided to begin maintenance work immediately, so between 1723 and 1729, side wings of the palace were constructed in place

General view of Queen Marie-Casimire's bedroom.

of the open galleries, harmonizing with the main block and vastly increasing the building's size. When her original architect, Giovanni Spazzio, died in 1726, his place was taken by Sigismund Deybel; the work itself was supervised by Józef Fontana. The new facades they created were adorned with stucco depictions of battles, allegorical figures, and scenes from Ovid's *Metamorphoses*. An orangery was built to Spazzio's plans and the gardens were extended northward. Inside the palace a number of frescoes were executed by a painter, Józef Rossi, and other walls were covered with huge mirrors and velvet tapestries.

Elżbieta's daughter Zofia, who became Princess Czartoryska on her

Ceiling fresco in Queen Marie-Casimire's bedroom portraying her as Aurora, late seventeenth century.

marriage in 1731, inherited Wilanów on her mother's death in 1729. With a mass of other commitments, she agreed to lease the palace to King Augustus II the Strong, who had repeatedly requested the arrangement, on the stipulation that nothing should be altered. Nevertheless the king had the south wing further extended, adding a large single-story dining room commissioned from Deybel. He moved in during 1731 and held court there with appropriate splendor for several weeks that summer. But his death two years later halted any other "improvements" he might have contemplated, and Zofia did not renew the lease to Augustus III. Instead, Wilanów was kept up with little done by way of alterations. Only the orangery was remodeled in mid-century and a late baroque stone parish church was erected in place of the old wooden one.

Zofia's daughter Izabela Lubomirska succeeded to Wilanów in 1771. For the preceding eighteen years she had been the chatelaine of Łańcut, and she had long before evinced her iron determination to get what she wanted. In 1775, then, she began her improvements by commissioning Szymon Bogumił Zug, who was also soon to begin building a villa for her at nearby Natolin. Zug first designed a bathhouse in neoclassical style to be added to Deybel's extension to the south wing. Here she created her own apartment, with an antechamber, salon, bedchamber, and bathroom, all luxuriously appointed. A new palace kitchen and guardhouse in the same style were constructed a little to the west. Inside the main house the walls of the entrance hall were marbled and decorated by Fryderyk Bauman. Izabela once more increased the size of the gardens, in 1784 instructing Zug to lay out an irregular garden in Anglo-Chinese taste with luxuriant vegetation, winding paths, and waterfalls. A team of gardeners was drafted, some of whom had been working on the landscape at Izabela Lubomirska's Mokotów garden near Warsaw, and under the supervision of the brothers Krystian and Godfryd Symon, the vegetable garden was reshaped in a rococo design, with linden trees and clipped hornbeams forming arbors with fountains, statues, and stone benches. Three alleys radiating from the palace's front gate were planted with lime trees.

When Izabela returned to Poland in 1789 after a long stay in France, she decided to settle as far away as possible from impending war or revolution. Since Łańcut seemed to offer the safest refuge, she decided to concentrate her collections there, emptying Wilanów and her residences in Warsaw of their contents, which were dispatched down the Vistula by barge. Her intuition of impending trouble was correct. In 1794 Tadeusz Kościuszko led an insurrection against the foreign powers occupying Poland during which Wilanów was stripped of its copper roofs and requisitioned for military purposes. Russian troops were later billeted there, and badly damaged both the palace and the gardens. Unwilling to return to her devastated property, Izabela handed it over in 1799 to her daughter Aleksandra, wife of Stanisław Kostka Potocki, a versatile scholar and a passionate collector.

For almost the next hundred years the Potockis were to own Wilanów, and they were to transform it lastingly. Stanisław Kostka's great aim was to reassemble as many Sobieski mementoes as possible, and while on countless trips to Western Europe he notably added to the palace's collections—in particular Chinese artifacts and antique vases (as a practicing archaeologist he also directed excavations himself) as well as paintings, all of which were to form the nucleus of the Wilanów gallery. Helped by his brother Ignacy, he also founded a magnificent library, which he installed within the superstructure of the belvedere. Wishing to open his treasures to the public, in 1805 Potocki established one of Poland's first museums in a neo-Gothic gallery especially designed by Chrystian Piotr Aigner as an extension of the north wing.

Stanisław Kostka's energies extended to the exterior too. Although the baroque parterres on the eastern side were left alone, he converted the rococo and Chinoiserie gardens created by his mother-in-law into an English-style landscape park. Follies and pavilions were added in the northern part of the garden: a Chinese summerhouse, a Roman bridge, and an ancient tomb with a mock triumphal arch. Potocki's multifarious interests also embraced cottage architecture and he was keen to improve the peasants' living conditions. He therefore designed new and more hygienic cottages, which gradually replaced the unhealthy old thatched hovels around the park. A hospital and village school were built as well to cater to the needs of the estate staff.

When Potocki died in 1821 his projects were faithfully continued by his widow and then by his son Aleksander. In 1836 the latter erected a neo-Gothic mausoleum to the memory of his parents in front of the palace gates, employing the sculptor Jakub Tatarkiewicz and the architect Enrico Marconi. The result was striking, even if it did not entirely blend in with its surroundings, but other refurbishment was less felicitous. From 1845 Franciszek Maria Lanci began reconstructing Aigner's neo-Gothic gallery, giving it a neo-Renaissance elevation with neorococo interiors. Izabela Lubomirska's bathhouse was substantially modified, and extra outbuildings were erected following Lanci's plans as well as a large stone pergola in the garden. Marconi then took over from Lanci, extending the hospital, building a chapel, and installing an ugly pump house down by the lake to supply water to the fountains.

Aleksander Potocki only lived until 1845, at which point Wilanów passed to his son August. He married his cousin Aleksandra, yet another Potocki, and she lived at Wilanów until 1892—for the last twenty-five of those years as a widow. Aleksandra became very much the controlling force on the property, adding new works of art to the collections and carrying on with the reconstruction of the palace. In this she was helped by Marconi's sons Władysław and Leandro, who had taken over his practice. During the 1870s a chamber for the family's antiquities was created in

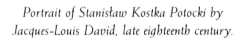

Portrait of Stanisław Kostka Potocki by Jacques-Louis David, late eighteenth century.

Interior of Izabela Lubomirska's bathroom.

the south gallery and another for their Etruscan artifacts in the north tower and the big library within the superstructure of the belvedere was redecorated. Yet again the parish church was altered as it acquired a lofty neobaroque dome.

With Aleksandra's death in 1892 the direct line of the family died out, so Wilanów was bequeathed to her nephew Ksawery Branicki. His ancestors had sprung to prominence in the Ukraine during the fifteenth century and had produced a leading Catholic bishop, a few grand hetmans, and a string of distinguished soldiers. One member had married Catherine the Great's illegitimate daughter and had fought a celebrated duel with Casanova; on capturing a notorious brigand named Ivan Gonda, this same Branicki had granted his prisoner's request to have his portrait painted before his execution and afterwards for it to hang in every subsequent Branicki's bedroom. Ksawery's grandfather had been part of the "Great Emigration" after the rising of 1831, departing to France where he had bought the chateau of Montrésor on the Loire; his father was a painter who regularly exhibited in the Paris Salon and lived there collecting pictures. After he had inherited Wilanów, Ksawery moved to Poland where he led a retiring life, augmenting the magnificent library and running his estates. Like his father and grandfather he financed scientific expeditions, in his case to Africa, Asia, and particularly the Caucasus; he also became a

The painting gallery arranged by Count August Potocki in the mid-nineteenth century.

Painting of King Jan Sobieski's former banqueting hall, converted into a library in the early nineteenth century, by Willibald Richter, mid-nineteenth century.

Count Adam Branicki in Polish national dress at a wedding, c. 1930. (Anna Branicka-Wolska.)

noted ornithologist. While he established a museum of national history in his Warsaw palace he eschewed politics, and although a chamberlain to the tsar, avoided going to the Saint Petersburg court.

Władysław Marconi was kept on as the consulting architect at Wilanów, and from 1893 embarked on another thirteen-year stint of reconstruction, primarily focused on the palace outbuildings this time, and with largely unfortunate results. By the early twentieth century the fabric of the building was starting to decay and there were various losses in the sculptural decorations. After World War I, when Adam Branicki had succeeded his father Ksawery, a restoration program was undertaken, but limited funds and mediocre workmanship meant that the underlying problems were not solved.

An amateur historian, Adam was also a devotee of Poland's national culture and a great supporter of the museum the family had established at Wilanów. The Potockis only lived in the south wing of the palace, leaving the north wing and central block as a museum, which, with the gardens, were regularly opened to the public. Like his father, Adam was essentially a private man who established a traditional, tranquil, and family-oriented life. His daughter Anna, in her recently published memoir, *Unposted Letters*, described Easters at Wilanów during her childhood in the 1930s. On the preceding Thursday the family would organize expeditions to the woods to gather violets, to the greenhouses for flowers, and to the kitchens to sample the food; on Good Friday, with no butter on their bread or sugar in their coffee, they went to church up to seven times to pray for redemption, and visited other churches in Warsaw in their Hispano Suiza to inspect the Easter crèches; and on Saturday huge tables laden with food were set up to be blessed by the priest—turkeys, glazed hams, and colored eggs alongside cakes bearing the word "Hallelujah" on their icing. Finally on Easter Day, after an early morning mass to celebrate the Resurrection, the household settled down to an enormous breakfast and to several days of merrymaking, entertaining innumerable friends and neighbors.

These happy days were rudely terminated by World War II. Germany's occupation of Poland led to the requisitioning of the palace, the removal of most of its contents, and the destruction of the gardens and many of their monuments. At length in 1943 the Branickis were evicted from Wilanów altogether and plans were made, luckily never realized, to turn it into an officers' club. After the Soviet takeover things were no better; Adam, who had already been imprisoned three times, was deported to Russia with his family in 1945 and returned three years later so worn out and emaciated that he died at a mere 55. His daughters were forbidden to live anywhere near their former home, or even to visit it.

Wilanów today seems to have banished these sad memories. After the contents looted by the Germans had been restored, in 1955 the Communist government at last began a thorough restoration, a process that took nine years and has brought the palace and its grounds back to their old splendor. In addition to the museums that Wilanów housed before the wars, a Polish portrait gallery has also been installed in one part of the palace. Clever restoration has removed most of the excrescences added in the nineteenth and twentieth centuries while allowing the best of the Lubomirski and Potocki alterations to remain. Externally and internally, Wilanów has been revealed again as the grand baroque residence of one of Poland's greatest kings.

NIEBORÓW
& ARKADIA

The landscape of Mazovia in central Poland is fairly flat and somewhat featureless, punctuated only by thick swathes of woodland. Nevertheless the area holds some unexpected and fascinating attractions, among them Fryderyk Chopin's delightful birthplace at Żelazowa Wola, west of Warsaw. Nearby and close to the pleasant town of Łowicz stands the small village of Nieborów. There, clearly visible through elegant railings and down a broad alley, rises an imposing chateau, the former residence of one of Poland's greatest noble families. And a mile or so further lies the entrance to its delightful pendant, the landscape garden of Arkadia.

The origins of Nieborów date from the late Middle Ages, when a group of yeoman farms first developed in the area. Embracing six neighboring villages and located near the old trade route from Warsaw to Poznań, used since the time of the Piast kings, the farms were gradually consolidated into one property, named like the main village after its founder, Niebor. By the early sixteenth century a family calling itself Nieborowski owned this property, and there just south of the road they built a two-story brick manor house decorated with many Gothic elements. To the north of the house stood the parish church, already in existence for over two centuries. No records of the house survive, although recent restoration work has shown that its large vaulted hall must have been positioned asymmetrically. There the Nieborowskis lived in respectable obscurity until they sold the estate in the early 1690s.

The purchaser was a far more significant figure, Cardinal Michał Stefan Radziejowski, archbishop of Gniezno and primate of Poland, who resided in nearby Łowicz. By 1695 he decided to build himself a magnificent chateau on the site and commissioned Tylman van Gameren, the royal architect, accordingly. The contrast with some of the more flamboyant buildings he designed in Warsaw was marked. Laying out his building on a rectangular plan, Tylman used the walls of the existing manor house but extended them at both ends, creating a long low edifice with twelve bays under a high copper roof. Two square alcove towers containing rooms, surmounted by finial-capped cupolas and protruding slightly, were added to flank the facade, a device often employed in Polish baroque architecture. The central four bays were framed by a pediment resting on unobtrusive pilasters. Internally the hall was realigned along the symmetrical axis of the new chateau, and a grand staircase led up to the state rooms on the upper floor. The garden, which stretched southward, derived from the formal French gardens then in fashion, with a canal, flat parterres, elaborate hedges, and thickets.

Before his new creation was even ready, the cardinal apparently tired of it, for in 1697 he presented Nieborów to his protégé, Jerzy Towiański,

Main facade of Nieborów, central Poland.

castellan of Łęczyca. The latter did not keep it for long, however—indeed over the ensuing seventy years the estate changed hands twice more. At length it was bought in 1766 by Michał Kazimierz Ogiński, grand hetman of Lithuania and palatine of Wilno. The new proprietor embarked forthwith on a major refurbishment of the neglected interiors. The main staircase was widened and its walls inlaid with Dutch tiles, while the Red Drawing Room, as it was called, and the adjoining bedchamber were redecorated in rococo taste. Much valuable furniture was brought in as well, and some splendid chimneypieces installed. In 1768 the pediment over the front door was filled with stucco carvings of war emblems, and in the middle a cartouche was created with the heraldic devices of Ogiński and his Czartoryski wife. A brick inn was also built just outside the front gates to improve the amenities of the village.

Despite his many talents as musician, poet, art patron, and entrepreneur (he was a backer of the Polesie Canal), Michał Kazimierz was not fated to enjoy his new property for long. In 1770 he joined with other malcontents and declared the deposition of King Stanisław August. Russian troops quickly crushed the rebels and, like many other magnates similarly placed, Ogiński fled into exile in Paris. Since he was unable to live at Nieborów any longer, he sold it in 1774 for four hundred thousand gold zlotys to his niece Helena Przeździecka and her husband, Michał Hieronim Radziwiłł.

After rising to prominence in Lithuania during the fifteenth century, the Radziwiłłs had played a major part in Polish history. Descended from the two cousins Mikołaj the Black and Mikołaj the Red—so-called in both cases for the respective color of their beards—they had regularly held many of the highest offices of state and had occasionally toyed with the idea of an independent Lithuanian state. The family owned the freehold of the enormous estates of Nieśwież and Ołyka, both of which were entailed and which conferred upon their holder the title of duke. The Radziwiłłs were also princes of the Holy Roman Empire and regarded themselves as quasi-independent, far better than the motley procession of Poland's kings. Their family pride, however, was tempered with hard-headed economic realism.

Michał Hieronim, then aged thirty and soon appointed palatine of Wilno, was a fairly typical Radziwiłł. Not overburdened with political scruples, he was one of the members of the Seym who duly recognized the First Partition of Poland in 1772, and as a member of the Confederation of Targowica in 1792, invited in the Russians again to suppress the

liberal reforms that had just been introduced. His chief concern was in making money, at which he succeeded brilliantly—for thirteen years in a row his annual income exceeded five million zlotys, much of it gained by administering the estates of Nieśwież and Ołyka for his young cousin Dominik Radziwiłł. Since the young head of the family was killed fighting with the Polish Legion in 1813 and left no heirs, Michał Hieronim was able to establish his own children's claim to the huge inheritance.

Helena, his wife, was equally ambitious in the social sphere, permanently engaged in friendly rivalry with Izabella Czartoryska over who should be the arbiter of taste and fashion in Warsaw. If her rival was to indulge in the new mania for landscape gardening, first at Powązki and then at Puławy, Helena was not to be left behind. Thus in 1778 the Radziwiłłs summoned Szymon Bogumił Zug to Nieborów. His brief was to extend the baroque garden, creating a promenade with alleys leading off it that would afford vistas of the new deer park established on the far side of the formal canal, the latter of which was now L-shaped with three pools and terraced slopes. Hothouses were erected, principally to shelter the large collection of orange trees brought from Dresden in the 1790s, and an earthen amphitheatre was also made. In addition Zug designed a complex of buildings near the chateau, including a coach house, stables, a brewery, estate offices, and a pavilion housing the main kitchen. On the other side of the public road a farmyard with a big central granary was also built.

But Helena aspired to more than just modernizing and improving the surroundings of Nieborów. She wanted to create an ideal rustic paradise, a place to escape from the frequently depressing realities of the age in Poland. The theories of Jean-Jacques Rousseau and the cult of the classical

and medieval worlds strongly informed the development of Arkadia, a romantic English-style landscape park she built only a mile or so from Nieborów. The name Arkadia derived from the pastoral region of ancient Greece, and had subsequently been used to describe a mythical isle where could be found the carefree bliss of an imaginary past. As she wrote, "You may call Arkadia an ancient monument to beautiful Greece. The traces of mythological worship, once preserved in art, are to be found here. The soul is overcome by a strong desire to express the feelings experienced, or those awakened in tender hearts by the mysterious charm of sacred groves."

In order to realize Helena's dream, Zug first dug an artificial lake christened the Big Pond. From there, steps led up to a Temple of Diana finished in 1783, a well-proportioned edifice with a portico of four columns and a semirotunda at the back surrounded by six Ionic pillars. Along the frieze ran a quote from Petrarch: *"Dove pace trovai d'ogni mia guerra"* ("Here I found peace after each struggle of mine"), while at the back appeared another inscription, this time from Horace: "I escape the others to find myself." Inside the temple, the walls of the central room were decorated with white stucco glazed to simulate marble, which contrasted effectively with the yellow Corinthian columns. The ceiling was painted by the French artist Jean-Pierre Norblin with a dramatic rendering of Aurora, goddess of the dawn, leading the horses of the sun god, Apollo. Next door in the so-called Etruscan study, depictions of utensils and

The aqueduct at Arkadia.

The Hermitage at Arkadia, designed by Szymon Bogumil Zug.

lamps were made in distemper on the plaster, while a ceiling fresco depicted a charmingly naive scene of Eros and Psyche. Guarded by a lion and a sphinx, the terrace provided views across the Big Pond to what was called the Isle of Feelings, where flowers were regularly placed on altars dedicated to love, friendship, gratitude, and memories. The grounds beyond were known as the Elysian Fields.

At one end of the Big Pond, Zug constructed a two-tiered, four-arched Roman Aqueduct. In a very different style he built a building called the High Priest's Sanctuary from brick and local ironstone. It contained fragments of friezes, moldings, frames, tablets, and armorial cartouches from the archbishop's castle at Łowicz and from tombs in the collegiate church there. To one side a columned terrace extended above an arched open vault. From 1795 to 1798 Zug constructed the Margrave's House, with its square battlemented tower approached through a wide brick and stone arch. Two herm heads and a lion mask were built into its walls and rosettes decorated the inside of one of the small doorways, all the work of the eminent Renaissance sculptor Jan Michałowicz.

By the dawn of the nineteenth century, neoclassical conventions were increasingly being discarded at Arkadia in favor of an eclectic Romantic style. About 1780 Zug built one of the first neo-Gothic edifices in Poland, a medieval-style house with twin spires designed by Aleksander Orłowski, a pupil of Norblin. Next to it the Sibyl's Grotto was created, its entrance framed by huge stones and a ruined altar picturesquely draped with bindweed and jasmine. Helena's tastes were growing ever more fanciful. Next she employed a young architect named Henryk Ittar who used marble, porphyry, and granite for his Tomb of Illusions, sited on the Poplar Isle in a stream, rechristened the River of Forgetfulness, which flowed out of the Big Pond. He also designed a circus for chariot racing and an amphitheatre, and although both were widely praised at the time, nothing of them has survived except for three obelisks in the circus.

General view of the library.

*Project for the reconstruction of Nieborów
by Giacomo Quarenghi, c. 1800.
(National Museum, Warsaw.)*

During these years Nieborów was not neglected either. In the 1780s Zug redecorated the rooms at the eastern end of the second floor in early neoclassical style. The chateau was filled with good furniture—English, French, and local—and with an impressive picture collection of both Old Masters and Polish portraits. The library contained twelve thousand books and two superlative globes from Venice, one terrestrial and one celestial, carved by Vincenzo Coronelli. Wishing to embellish the severe external appearance of the building, Helena commissioned Giacomo Quarenghi, later famous for his work at Saint Petersburg, although his grandiose new plans were never executed. The gardens were further remodeled *à l'anglaise*, with a wide variety of tree species being planted and more alleys cut through the lime woods, one of which terminated in a ha-ha, the name given to the hidden, semicircular projection over the ditch. Sculpture of all kinds from Europe and Asia, including figures, bas-reliefs, columns with inscriptions in Greek and Arabic, and sarcophagi, were scattered around the gardens as if to emphasize their owners' cosmopolitan identity.

The Radziwiłłs adapted very skillfully to the extinction of the Polish state under the partition. Their eldest son, Ludwik, was sent to Saint Petersburg where he obtained a commission in the Russian army, while his son Leon was later appointed aide-de-camp to the tsar. Helena contrived to marry off her second son, Antoni, to Princess Louise of Prussia, niece of Frederick the Great, and from this union, a genuine love-match, the future senior line of the family would spring. Her father, King Frederick William II, intimated that a generous wedding settlement would be welcome, so Antoni's famously parsimonious father bought him a magnificent residence in Berlin and an estate in the Prussian zone of occupied Poland where an unusual wooden house, named after him and designed by Karl Friedrich Schinkel, would one day be built. A Maecenas of music and the arts, Antoni wrote the first musical score for Goethe's *Faust* and

Empire chair in the study at Nieborów.

became the friend and patron of Chopin. His appointment in 1818 as viceroy of the Grand Duchy of Poznań, which the Prussians had created from the Polish territory they had annexed, suggests how greatly respected he was by the Russian government, a status further enhanced by being granted Nieśwież and Ołyka by the tsar.

The Radziwiłłs' third son, Michał Gedeon, was a complete contrast. A liberal who fought in Kościuszko's uprising, he subsequently accompanied Helena to Paris where he became an enthusiastic supporter of Napoleon. When the French created the duchy of Warsaw, he was given command of one of its infantry regiments, and he later served with distinction as a brigadier in the War of 1812. After 1815 he married and was made a senator in the Congress Kingdom. When the remarkable Helena died in 1821, ten years before her long-lived husband, Michał Gedeon inherited the properties of Nieborów and Szpanów. But ten years later he was forced to flee abroad and his estates were confiscated after his having accepted the post of commander-in-chief of the Polish forces during the suppressed revolt against Russia. Only through the family's intercession at Saint Petersburg were the properties offered to their Russified cousin Leon Radziwiłł, who generously gave them back again a few years afterward to Michał Gedeon's sons, still minors. Their father was eventually allowed to return

Grotesque head with foliage painted by Szymon Mankowski.

Neo-rococo boudoir.

Armorial stove produced in the Nieborów workshops, c. 1885.

and lived in reduced state at Nieborów, for the property had been damaged in the fighting and there were numerous creditors demanding satisfaction. His masterful wife, Aleksandra, provided the real impetus to keep up the estate, and after her husband's death in 1850 she set about restoring the chateau and gardens, redecorating the White Salon in late neoclassical taste.

Trouble struck when her elder son, Zygmunt, took charge on her death in 1864. A hopeless spendthrift and entirely uninterested in the character of his inheritance, he removed the whole of the library to Paris where it was sold at auction. In constant need of money, he disposed of numerous works of art too, and even put the neglected Arkadia up for sale. He finally decided to settle in France, and in 1879 agreed to sell Nieborów to his brother's son Michał Piotr.

Luckily the new proprietor, an active philanthropist who endowed many orphanages and led a busy public life, was to prove a far worthier figure than his profligate uncle. Restoration recommenced, and in 1886 Leandro Marconi, son of the distinguished architect Enrico, was commissioned to alter the chateau both inside and out. The results were not wholly felicitous. The insertion over the front door of three tall closely spaced windows plus a balcony destroyed the external proportions of the building. The main vaulted hall was given heavy oak, pseudo-Renaissance wainscoting and an overly ornate fireplace, while several of the state rooms at the western end of the second floor were refurbished in elaborate neo-rococo taste. The medieval parish church was demolished and replaced with the neo-Gothic edifice that still stands today. But Michał Piotr also set up joinery workshops at Nieborów and Szpanów, which produced badly needed furniture for the chateau. Moreover in 1881 he established a majolica works, which intermittently over the next twenty-five years produced a stream of tiled stoves, plates, candlesticks, jugs, vases, lamps, and wall tiles; in its final phase under the direction of the outstanding potter Stanisław Jagmin, it also turned out decorative pieces in an art nouveau style.

Since Michał Piotr was childless, he decided before his death in 1906 to bequeath Nieborów to his cousin's son Janusz, the great-grandson of Antoni. Having just acquired a bride, Anna Lubomirska, Janusz wished to make a comfortable home, but he did not find Nieborów large enough for the needs of the age, with its enormous staffs and elaborate house parties. Two schemes to add wings to the front of the chateau were under consideration when World War I intervened. In 1915 Józef Piłsudski's Polish Legion skirmished against the Russians in the neighborhood, and Arkadia, with several of the pavilions, was damaged in the fighting. Fortunately Nieborów itself escaped unscathed, although both sides did a limited amount of plundering. Curiously, all of the eighteenth-century carriages were requisitioned during the war and, of course, never returned.

In the newly-independent postwar Poland, Janusz Radziwiłł found himself one of the nation's largest landowners. His properties included Szpanów and Nieborów, with nearly twenty-five thousand acres, along with Ołyka, an immense and beautiful castle located to the east in Volhynia, with a courtyard larger than the Piazza San Marco, over two hundred rooms, and a landholding still amounting to nearly eighty thousand acres. His eldest son was furthermore to marry his distant cousin Izabela, daughter of the line that owned the still larger Nieśwież estates. All lay within the post-1919 frontiers.

Despite being such a large landowner, Janusz was an active politician and close associate of Piłsudski's who preferred to spend most of his time in his Warsaw palace or within easy reach of the capital. Since Nieborów was relatively near, plans to enlarge it were pursued. In 1922 the architect Romuald Gutt created a third floor by converting the spacious attic into guest bedrooms, covering the roof with tiles instead of copper plate, which permitted the insertion of windows in it. The ground floor, too, was reconstructed in 1929–30: at one end a smoking room and a dining room were created, while at the other Janusz made his offices. The chateau's furnishings were completed, to a great extent with eighteenth-century copies, and more paintings were brought in. They, along with the rest of the Radziwiłłs' collections, were readily made available to scholars. The front drive was also changed to enable a large lawn to be made along the main facade, and baroque lion statues now guarded it.

Within a fortnight of the outbreak of World War II, in mid-September 1939, the area round Nieborów became the scene of heavy German-Polish fighting, although once more the buildings were not damaged. Janusz happened to be at Ołyka at the time and after the Russian invasion was deported to the Soviet Union with his family. Thanks to high-level intervention, he was released that December and returned to Poland, where he immersed himself in welfare work for his compatriots. With large forests and strategic railway lines in the vicinity, Nieborów was a center for Resistance activity, in which his elder son and daughter-in-law participated. In consequence the population suffered from German reprisals—indeed some of the estate staff were shot or sent to concentration camps. Later the chateau was turned into a German headquarters and a committee of Nazi art historians confiscated nineteen crates of the best contents, although these were mostly recovered after the war.

Portrait of Duke Janusz Radziwiłł by Waclawa Radwana, 1920.

Radziwiłł family reunion for Princess Mary
Radziwiłł's eightieth birthday, 1980s.
(Princess Mary Radziwiłł.)

Although he had refused all offers to cooperate with the Nazis, Janusz was nevertheless rearrested by the Soviets in 1945, and in company with other aristocrats who had sought refuge at his home—sundry Branickis, Krasińskis, and Zamoyskis—he was taken off to captivity in Russia. Just before his return almost three years later, his wife died in prison, but he survived until 1967, living in a tiny flat in Warsaw. Nieborów and Arkadia had meanwhile been declared a branch of the National Museum in February 1945 and opened to the public, later becoming a conference center and retreat for intellectuals. Major restoration work on the chateau from 1966 to 1970 has left the interiors in good condition, while the outbuildings, gardens, and park have been well maintained. At Arkadia the garden layout with its large pond and streams has been recreated, but some of the buildings are still in urgent need of renovation.

The appeal of Nieborów and Arkadia does not lie solely in the fine architecture and decoration found at the former, nor in the status of the latter as perhaps the most completely preserved Romantic landscape in Poland. It is also their connection for nearly two centuries with one of the country's greatest noble dynasties, and with one exceptional woman in particular, who substantially brought into being what we see today. As Helena Radziwiłł's inscription by the entrance gate puts it, "Oh you sweet land of Arkadia, more sweet to me than any other. I touch you with my feet and with my thoughts I welcome you."

PUŁAWY & GOŁUCHÓW

*F*ollowing the interesting minor road that runs southeast from Warsaw toward Lublin and parallel to the Vistula River, after a hundred kilometers or so the small town of Puławy appears. This enjoys an historic fame out of all proportion either to its size or to the massive and undistinguished chateau it contains. For here lived the Czartoryskis, one of the most important families in Poland and the creators at Puławy of a patriotic shrine and a wonderful landscape garden. Some seventy years after the family fled from Puławy a daughter of this same aristocratic dynasty was responsible for transforming another chateau called Gołuchów, far to the west in Wielkopolska, into a museum with the similar purpose of preserving Polish culture.

In the seventeenth century Puławy was a fishing village on the Vistula, which Zofia Opalińska, the first bride of Stanisław Herakliusz Lubomirski, brought with her as her dowry. On this site Lubomirski commissioned his favorite architect, Tylman van Gameren, to build a baroque villa in 1671, a residence of considerable charm, as the surviving drawings show. In 1702 the property passed to his daughter Elżbieta, who had married Adam Sieniawski, future grand hetman of the crown. Unfortunately the villa was burned down by the Swedish troops of King Charles XII only four years later, and it was not until 1722 that Elżbieta Sieniawska began its reconstruction, a task continued by her daughter Zofia, who inherited Puławy before her marriage to Prince August Czartoryski in 1731. For over fifty years the couple spent most of their summers at the property, and during that time transformed it into one of the principal artistic monuments of Poland.

When most of the work was complete by 1736, the villa had grown into an imposing baroque chateau whose wings surrounded a large cour d'honneur and a fountain. The two eminent architects involved were Giovanni Spazzio and, after his death, Sigismund Deybel. Yet the end product was not inspired, for the chateau, although large, was heavy and undistinguished, unrelieved by any flashes of originality. The best facade, which overlooked the river, displayed Doric pilasters above a rusticated basement and entered onto a fine rococo pillared entrance hall. Italian stuccodores were employed, and the Frenchman Juste-Aurèle Meissonier was instructed to design the interior of the polygonal Golden Salon on the second floor. The fittings of this rococo room were made in Paris during the 1730s and later shipped to Poland; tradition also claimed that François Boucher painted the ceiling. A large park with geometric alleys in the French style was also laid out, and a succession of skillful gardeners proceeded to fill it in. Several pavilions were built on the grounds. By the mid-eighteenth century Puławy had become a center of artistic activity, home to the studios of the painter Sebastian Zeisel and the Hoffman family of sculptors.

Puławy seen from beyond the fountain, eastern Poland.

Watercolor of Marynka Palace at Puławy by Zygmunt Vogel, late eighteenth century. (National Museum, Warsaw.)

Portrait of Izabella Czartoryska by Kazimierz Wojniakowski, c. 1796. (Czartoryski Museum, Kraków.)

Portrait of Adam Kazimierz Czartoryski in the costume of the general of Podolia, by Louis Mathieu, c. 1790. (Czartoryski Museum, Kraków.)

A seminal date in Puławy's evolution was 1782, the year Prince August died and was succeeded by his son Adam Kazimierz Czartoryski. A man of nearly fifty, highly educated with wide historical, literary, and classical interests, he avoided a public career of his own, preferring instead to mediate between the Familia, as the Czartoryskis' cabal of friends and relations was known, and other groups of aristocratic politicians who wielded power in eighteenth-century Poland. Although he now disagreed politically with his cousin the king, he supported all Stanisław August's cultural iniatives. Furthermore he was blessed with a remarkable wife. Rich and intelligent, Izabella was the daughter of Jerzy Flemming, the treasurer of Lithuania. She had married Adam Kazimierz, who was her mother's cousin, aged a mere fifteen, and originally her marriage was not happy. She traveled widely, enjoying the frivolous, cosmopolitan life of the Ancien Régime, but she was always interested in the arts, and by 1785 was commissioning further work at Puławy. Her architect, Chrystian Piotr Aigner, first designed an orangery in a Doric Greek style, soon followed by the little neoclassical Marynka Palace intended for her daughter.

Izabella enthusiastically espoused the nationalist cause, as did her husband in characteristically restrained fashion, so when Kościuszko's rising had been crushed, the Czartoryskis faced the full force of Russian vengeance. Their estates were declared forfeit, although this was subsequently reversed, and her two sons were packed off to Saint Petersburg to ensure the family's good behavior. Puławy had been thoroughly pillaged by Catherine the Great's troops both inside and in the park. Izabella's emotional energetic nature reacted violently: henceforward she would dedicate her life and energies to the nationalist cause, and it was in this spirit that she began renovating Puławy in 1796. Her intention was not just to renovate, but rather to create a patriotic museum. As she wrote, "It was when Poland ceased to exist that the idea came to me to gather together all manner of Polish mementoes and bequeath them to posterity. A person who loses a mother or child holds dear those objects they have left behind, and although these mementoes evoke sorrow, their sight also brings relief."

Aigner was instructed to build a model of the Roman Temple of the Sibyl at Tivoli on a site overlooking the Vistula. Each of its two stories consisted of a circular hall; the lower level was so set back into the hillside as to be accessible only from the river front, while viewed from the chateau the upper floor resembled a single-story domed peripteral rotunda. The upper hall's stuccoed white walls formed a smooth cylindrical surface

beneath a frieze of griffins and a coffered dome, which was encircled by 18 columns with composite capitals. Over the high double doors of its portal was inscribed, *"Przeszłość-Przyszłości"* ("The Past to the Future"). The lower hall had vaulting supported by thick buttresses, and nine pillars formed a central aisle. Originally entitled the Temple of Memory, the building was soon rechristened the Temple of Sibyl and combined pagan architecture with such Christian motifs as the apse being turned east. When completed it was crammed with a variety of military trophies, souvenirs, or relics of national heroes ranging from King Bolesław the Brave to Copernicus the astronomer.

From 1800 to 1803 Aigner was also busy constructing a church modeled on the Pantheon in Rome, in which Ionic columns carried an airy gallery in the charming interior. And his patron Izabella was dreaming of another museum pavilion as a depository for curiosities she had acquired on her foreign travels. So Aigner created a building called the Gothic House, based on an existing structure and with walls of brick and stone. These were inset with over three hundred tablets and inscriptions, while the six rooms inside contained a diversity of exhibits emphasizing chivalry, heroism, and the struggle for liberty. Izabella then transformed the formal French gardens into a landscape park *à l'anglaise* spread along both sides of the Vistula. Grottoes were built above the river bank, picturesquely-sited clumps of trees were planted, and vistas were created between the chateau and pavilions. Her widely acclaimed *Treatise on Gardening* showed her deep love for and knowledge of the subject. Although her husband was relatively uninvolved with the extraordinary revival of Puławy after 1794, Adam Kazimierz did reestablish the splendid library that the Czartoryskis had assembled, and installed a printing press and a lithographic workshop on the estate.

As a middle-aged man, Adam Jerzy inherited Puławy on his father's death in 1823. He had been the chief progenitor of the Congress Kingdom, but his growing alienation from Tsar Alexander I persuaded him to withdraw substantially from politics in order to concentrate on writing and his new family, for he had married late in life. Although many years before he had bought important pictures including a Raphael, a Leonardo, and a Rembrandt for the family collection, he had never found the time to devote to patronage of the arts. Now he began a collection of scientific books for the library and settled down to running his estates, although his octogenarian mother was still extremely active.

Nemesis arrived in 1830. After the collapse of the uprising of 1830–31 during which Adam Jerzy had headed the provisional government, the vengeful Russians again attacked Puławy. The family had already closed the museum and library and hidden their exhibits. Now a full evacuation was ordered, and, supervised by the indomitable Izabella, the contents were removed for safety to neighboring churches, monasteries, and the Zamoyski residences of Klemensów and Kozłówka. Russian troops captured part of the library while the rest was brought down the Vistula in boats under heavy fire. Izabella and her daughter fled to the Czartoryski estate at Sieniawa in Austrian-occupied Galicia, taking the choicest articles from the Temple of Sibyl with them. When tsarist officials arrived to sequestrate the property, they found both chateau and museum empty. This time, however, the decree was not to be rescinded. A school called the Alexandrian Institute for the Education of Young Women was transferred to Puławy, to be succeeded by an agricultural institute. The chateau underwent some immediate rebuilding, and more in the 1840s after a fire had damaged it badly. The interior was inevitably destroyed by degrees, but the park landscape and pavilions of the grandiloquently renamed "New Alexandria" remained intact.

Although their connection with Puławy had been severed forever, this was not the end of the Czartoryskis or of their collections. The family still owned large estates in Galicia, the part of Poland annexed by Austria, and Adam Jerzy had escaped to western Europe. Condemned to death in absentia, he settled in Paris where he became head of a government in exile, "an uncrowned king," as he was reckoned, although his policies and diplomacy were condemned as useless by the radical emigrés. In 1843 he managed to buy the dilapidated Hotel Lambert, a grand seventeenth-century building by Louis Le Vau on the Île Saint-Louis, which became his headquarters. He financed journals, a Polish library, and various charitable institutions for his compatriots, and every year a ball plus a fair was held for the emigré community in the tented-over courtyard. On the façade was carved the optimistic inscription: *Le Jour viendra.*

Adam Jerzy's children, in particular his younger son Władysław and daughter Izabela, took on the mantle of his leadership in the Polish emigré community; they had also inherited their grandmother's mania for collecting. Władysław, born in 1828 and married to a distant relation of the Spanish royal house, displaced his sickly elder brother as heir to the family traditions, especially after his father died aged 91 in 1861. An art connoisseur, he assembled a fine collection of Flemish and Italian primitive paintings, objects d'art, oriental pieces, silverwork, glass, porcelain, textiles, and miniatures, as well as a range of classical objects. In 1865 a portion of these treasures were exhibited in a major French exhibition and received high praise from the critics. Nevertheless, he still dreamed of reassembling the Czartoryski collections on Polish soil. Finally in 1876 Władysław reached an agreement with the Kraków city council, which offered him several buildings, principally the former arsenal, for a museum. He accepted the offer, commissioning Maurice-Auguste Ouradou to redesign the interiors, but since his library took up most of the available space, it became necessary to buy an old monastery as well, which was similarly adapted. The result was a triumph. Many of the Puławy treasures, like the commanders' shields from the Temple of Sibyl, were reassembled, while the splendid collection of paintings, including the Raphael, Leonardo, and Rembrandt, excited universal admiration. The Emperor Francis Joseph even paid a visit, and the Austrian government, which had now conceded substantial autonomy to Galicia, where the Czartoryskis' Sieniawa estates were located, allowed them to form an entail with provision made for the maintenance of the museum and library. The Kraków collections stayed as a private foundation until 1945, when they were taken under state control, but since they were never actually nationalized, their legal status has remained equivocal.

Portrait of Adam Jerzy Czartoryski by Leon Kaplinski, 1860. (Kórnik collection.)

View of Sieniawa, southeastern Poland, the third of the Czartoryskis' houses. (Prince Adam Czartoryski.)

Temple of Sibyl at Puławy.

Watercolor of the Temple of Sibyl, by Zygmunt Vogel, late eighteenth century. (Kórnik collection.)

His sister Izabela married Jan Działyński in 1857, whose father, Tytus, had been instrumental in getting out some of the family's treasures, large numbers of which found their way from Poland to France. Tytus was himself no minor collector, and his son Jan followed in his footsteps, turning their neo-Gothic castle of Kórnik, near Poznań, into an important library and museum collection. In 1853 Tytus had bought the ruined castle of Gołuchów, also in Wielkopolska northeast of Kalisz, which four years later he presented to his son on his marriage. But the young couple scarcely lived there to begin with, and after 1863, when Jan was condemned to death for his part in the revolt against Russian rule, they were forced to flee abroad.

Gołuchów's history was already several centuries old, the earliest parts of the castle having been built around 1560 for Rafał Leszczyński. A leading Protestant, chancellor of Poland, and spokeman for the executionist movement, he had commissioned a square, three-story fortified keep with four octagonal corner towers. His son Wacław became chancellor too, and after inheriting the castle in 1592, proceeded to convert it into a splendid magnate's residence. A one-story dwelling house plus a loggia and a hexagonal tower were built south of the courtyard and connected to the main block by two short wings. But the Leszczyńskis' star waned during the seventeenth century, at the end of which they sold the property. For 150 years Gołuchów stood empty, for none of the many succeeding owners ever lived in it, and by the mid-nineteenth century it was almost totally derelict.

When the confiscation decree on Jan Działyński's estates was revoked, he gave the castle to his wife Izabela in 1872 in consideration of various debts he owed her. Originally she had not liked Gołuchów but slowly she came to love it, christening it "her paradise on earth." It was her restoration that gave Gołuchów its present-day appearance. With her French education, she had at first consulted the celebrated architect Eugène

Prince Władysław Czartoryski and his son Adam, c. 1880. (Czartoryski Museum, Kraków.)

Watercolor of Gołuchów by Jan Kopczynski, l nineteenth century. (Kórnik collection.)

Gołuchów seen from the park.

Viollet-le-Duc, who recommended Ouradou, his own son-in-law and pupil. The latter chose not to reconstruct the Renaissance castle; rather, he transformed it in the fashionable style of the sixteenth century, modeled on the Loire chateaux—hence the slate roofs, the narrow chimneys, and the sculptural decoration so typical of the period. Most of the courtyard's sculptures have a genuine French or Italian provenance, even though other features are straight copies, such as the staircase, which is copied from the Bargello in Florence. The restoration, lasting from 1875 to 1885, preserved some of the original parts of the castle. The north terrace of the courtyard lay above the sixteenth-century cellars, while three of the towers and the foundations of the belvedere also survived from the earlier structure.

Izabela's purpose in all this was entirely deliberate. She wanted to re-create a sixteenth-century Polish royal residence, and not merely because of the Czartoryskis' past connections with the throne. In an era of enforced Germanization, she intended to challenge Prussian authority by establishing a museum collection of international importance emphasizing her country's cultural heritage. Like her grandmother at Puławy, she required that everything about Gołuchów, both architecture and contents, must be worthy of this goal. The inscription above the main entrance encapsulated her aims: *"Vito dei cadunt, surgunt, resurgunt aedesque regnaque"* ("By God's will kingdoms and buildings rise, fall and rise again"). The Leszczyński device and the royal crown can be found throughout the house. The Polish and Museum Halls along with the Spanish and Italian Rooms, a drawing room, a dining room, and a state bedroom comprised a magnificent ensemble, which displayed Izabela's treasures in a spirit of eclectic historicism.

Jan Działyński died in 1880. Although he had been responsible for laying out the fine landscape park at Gołuchów, he lived his last years at Kórnik. His widow survived him by nineteen years, building unsightly

Chapel in the park at Gołuchów.

Interior of the library at Gołuchów.

Izabela Działyńska (née Czartoryska), late nineteenth century.

Wedding of August Czartoryski and Princess
Marie Dolores of Bourbon-Orleans at Sieniawa,
1937. (Prince Adam Czartoryski.)

residential quarters elsewhere in the park to enable the castle to function purely as a museum; a nearby chapel was also erected to her memory shortly after her death. Her nephew and great-nephew, Władysław Czartoryski's younger son and grandson, successively inherited Gołuchów during the next four decades. It continued uninterrupted as a museum until September 1939, when, after the German occupation, the exhibits were seized. Many were lost, stolen, or exported, although the wonderful collection of antique vases was returned after World War II. Izabela had created an entail that guaranteed the indivisibility of the property and public access to the collections, but now the state expropriated Gołuchów and the administration was given to the Poznań National Museum.

Both Puławy and Gołuchów are of great interest to any student of Poland's political and cultural heritage. The visual charms of both are somewhat limited—one, although a fine museum, is too much of a pastiche of a Loire chateau, while the other has served institutional purposes for more than a century and therefore lacks its original charm. Yet the beauty of Puławy's park and pavilions along with the extraordinary diversity of Gołuchów's exhibits combine to provide an imperishable memorial to one of Poland's greatest families.

Ł A Z I E N K I

South of the city center of Warsaw lies a large and beautiful park called Łazienki, a Polish equivalent of Hyde Park, Central Park, and the Bois de Boulogne. Although it was originally built as a country retreat, Warsaw has grown to the point that today the park is very much in the urban area. Little is visible from the roads that run along its perimeter aside from the imposing Belvedere Palace, now the residence of the country's president. Hidden within thick clumps of trees, however, stand a number of delightful pavilions and monuments, the chief of which, now known as the Palace-on-the-Water, must rank among the architectural jewels of Europe.

The history of Łazienki began simply enough during the Middle Ages when the dukes of Mazovia, rulers of one of the petty principalities into which Poland was then divided, built a castle they called Ujazdów on the escarpment of the Vistula River some two miles south of Warsaw. During the thirteenth century it was twice burned down—once during a Lithuanian invasion and once in the course of a civil war. By the sixteenth century a wooden house belonging to Queen Bona's daughter Anna Jagiellonka had been constructed down near the river and close to the site of the medieval castle. Here in 1578 the wedding of Chancellor Jan Zamoyski to Krystyna Radziwiłł took place, at which the first Polish drama, *Odprawa Posłów Greckich* (*The Dismissal of the Greek Envoys*) was performed. In 1624 the Vasa king Zygmunt III built a quadrangular, two-storied brick castle with corner towers and an arcaded loggia where the old fortress had stood. The architect, Matteo Castelli, followed the plans of Giovanni Trevano.

After the wooden house was decimated and the castle partially destroyed during "the Swedish Deluge," as the Swedish invasion of Poland in the mid-seventeenth century was known, the Ujazdów estate was bought in 1674 by Stanisław Herakliusz Lubomirski, grand marshal of the crown, patron of the arts, writer, and philosopher. Some time before 1690 he commissioned his protégé, the Dutch architect Tylman van Gameren, to build two pavilions for him on the wooded marshy land where a menagerie had previously been located. In one of them, called the Hermitage—a small, square, one-story building with a mansard roof—Lubomirski was wont to retire from the travails of public life. The other structure, the Bathhouse (or Łaźnia in Polish), stood on a rectangular islet surrounded on three sides by canals and on the fourth by a symmetrical pond. This luxurious and spacious pavilion was built on a square plan with a pedimented and pilastered north elevation rising through two stories. Externally its severe lines were relieved by three cupolas, the larger central one forming a dome over an internal rotunda, which was illuminated through a lantern. Inside, the Bathhouse was richly decorated in what was described at the time as "the grotesque taste." The building's rotunda had a fountain in the middle and walls studded with shells and pebbles to create the illusion of a grotto. Off this chamber led a bathing apartment with a cascade, twin tin tubs, and a good number of rest chambers.

After Lubomirski's death King Augustus II the Strong leased the Ujazdów

General view of the Palace-on-the-Water at Łazienki, near Warsaw.

Old view of the Palace-on-the-Water, by Zygmunt Vogel, late eighteenth century. (National Museum, Warsaw.)

Portrait of King Stanisław II August, by Marcello Bacciarelli, late eighteenth century.

estate from the grand marshal's heirs in 1720 and built a large canal along what had been the axis of Castelli's castle. He envisaged a grandiose reconstruction of the building and had plans drawn up by Matthias Daniel Pöppelmann, architect of the Zwinger palace in Dresden. But the plans were never realized, and for the next forty years little was done to the property. In 1764, however, Ujazdów was bought by Stanisław August Poniatowski, who would be elected that same year as Poland's last king. The great age of the estate was about to begin.

Work began almost immediately. The king had an entrance avenue laid out some three miles in length, leading from the city to Ujazdów. Within the park a star-shaped grid was developed of straight alleys lined with linden trees, a concept derived from French models. Under Lubomirski the largely-ruined Ujazdów castle had undergone a limited restoration by Tylman van Gameren, who had created some baroque interiors, but from 1766 King Stanisław August began adding another story and refurbishing the interiors. His chief court architect, Domenico Merlini, provided the designs, while the artists Bernardo Bellotto and Franciszek Smuglewicz provided most of the interior painted decoration. A new facade was also erected as well as large side pavilions. Yet the king found the resulting architectural hotchpotch inharmonious. Additionally it was too small for the court, and by 1775 he had ceased to live there. Nine years later it was converted into a monumental classicist army barracks by Stanisław Zawadzki and remained in this service the rest of its life, even serving as a military hospital in this century before being burned out during World War II. The reconstructed castle is a twentieth-century copy of its seventeenth-century forebear.

After abandoning the castle, in the summer of 1775 the king moved into the partially-remodeled Łaźnia or Bathhouse, which was soon to become known as the Palace-on-the-Water in reference to its location on a small islet. Finding once more a lack of space, the king made a dining room out of his ground-floor bedroom and there held his Thursday dinners, gatherings noted for their conversational brilliance and attended by writers and scholars. His move to the second floor meant that further rooms had to be added there. On either side of the building small Chinese galleried bridges covered with green and gilt roofs were constructed to link the islet on which the little palace was situated to the mainland.

The end product was still unsatisfactory, however, so in 1784 a third re-building by Merlini replaced the south facade with a recessed portico framed by four composite columns. Four years later the other three fronts acquired classical facades too, the northern one being given thirteen bays of the same colossal order and a pedimented portico. Further work in 1792 produced two lateral pavilions on the mainland linked to the main block of the building by stone bridges with colonnaded galleries. At last the various parts of the structure were harmonized, the pilastered eleva-tions crowned by a flat sculpture-lined attic. The belvedere rising from the middle section gave an elegant flourish to the whole ensemble and signaled the erstwhile bath pavilion's transformation into a miniature pal-ace. Along the roofs, statuary by André Le Brun was installed repre-senting the four elements, the four continents then known, and the four seasons, while the north portico's pediment was filled with the seated fig-ures of Fame and Peace. The inscription on a baroque cartouche above the entrance read: *"Haec domus odit tristitias, amit pacem, fundat balnea, commen-dat rura et optat probos"* ("This house hates sadness, loves peace, offers baths, recommends rural life and welcomes the virtuous").

Inside, three rooms retained their baroque features: the vestibule, the tile-paneled Bacchus room, and the bathing apartment, where only the tin tubs and the cascade were removed. By contrast the purely neoclassi-cal ballroom, designed by Jan Chrystian Kamsetzer on a simple rectangu-lar plan, was decorated with painted panels of warm red-and-brown–toned

Ballroom by Jan Chrystian Kamsetzer in the Palace-on-the-Water.

grotesques by Jerzy Bogumił Plersch. The closely hung picture gallery and Merlini's Solomon Hall were added in the rebuilding of 1788. Although the latter is more exuberant, featuring Marcello Bacciarelli's huge paintings of biblical and allegorical subjects, it displays fine architectural proportions as well. The rotunda, which became the only chamber to survive the destruction of World War II virtually unscathed, was the object of Stanisław August's last alteration to the palace. This room he redecorated as a sort of national pantheon, with monumental statues of Poland's four greatest kings in niches, and busts of Roman emperors set above the doors. Interestingly, all of the rooms in the Palace-on-the-Water were of different heights; the dining room, for instance, was around ten feet high, while the gallery was perhaps two-and-a-half feet taller and the rotunda maybe five feet taller than that.

The residential rooms on the second floor had originally been constructed on a more intimate scale, and they remained that way. With the picture gallery and the portrait study on the ground level, they alone contained paintings on canvas. The fine royal collection contained many Dutch works including six Rembrandts, and such contemporary French masters as Pierre Fragonard and Hubert Robert. Many more were assembled for the king in London, but since after his abdication he was in no position to pay for them they remained in England and became the nucleus of the Dulwich Picture Gallery in London. Elsewhere in the palace, murals and stucco work carried symbolic representations of the virtues or of human fate and greatness, providing a decorative backdrop to the opulence of the marble, bronze, and gilding. At the beginning the furniture, clocks, and porcelain all came from Paris, but gradually Stanisław August commissioned pieces by Polish craftsmen.

Unable to accommodate his guests, the king at first had an inn built near the park entrance, followed in 1775 by a pyramidal guardhouse, which was demolished early in the following century. That same year a

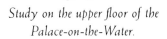

*Study on the upper floor of the
Palace-on-the-Water.*

Detail of wall frescoes in the White House.

*Bedroom in the White House furnished with King
Stanisław August's bed; the paintings on the walls
are by Jerzy Bogumił Plersch and Jan Scisko, late
eighteenth century.*

square villa called the White House was completed, built to Merlini's plans. The king may originally have intended it for himself, but he soon gave it to his mistress, Elżbieta Grabowska; his sisters later lived there too. Entirely regular externally with four identical elevations, an attic, and a small belvedere on the roof, the structure was designed in early neo-classical style, although the first-floor segmental window arches harked back to the rococo. In contrast to the building's regular exterior, all the rooms were of a different shape. Plersch, the principal decorator, covered the dining room with his grotesque compositions, while the drawing room contains big mural views of China, which, with the adjacent bed-room, are the sole remaining remnants of Chinoiserie taste so much in evidence at Łazienki in the days of Stanisław August. Arranged around a central staircase, all the rooms have survived virtually intact from the period.

In 1777 Stanisław August remodeled Lubomirski's Hermitage, which had been struck by lightning, and gave it as a residence to his confidante, the fortune-teller Madame Lhullier. From 1775–78 he also had Merlini occupied with constructing a new palace called the Myślewice. Initially planned as a square like the White House, it had two semicircular wings added even before completion to give it a horseshoe shape. Although it was intended to house the royal court, the king soon handed it over to his nephew Józef Poniatowski, future marshal and hero of the Napoleonic Wars, whose initials appear above the front door. A reservoir was also built, a cylindrical structure modeled on the tomb of Cecilia Metella near Rome, with no exterior openings but miniature rooms looking onto a tiny courtyard.

The king's work on Łazienki, as the entire complex was now called, continued through the 1770s and into the 1780s. Finished in 1780 and de-signed in the Chinese style, the Trou-Madame pavilion was named for a game akin to billiards, which consisted of throwing metal balls into numbered goals. Within two years it was transformed into a small theatre. By 1788 however, a far larger one seating two hundred spectators was available in the east wing of Merlini's Orangery, with nine boxes at second-floor level separated by female figures holding candelabra that stand between pairs of pilasters. A circular ceiling mural was created for the theatre by Plersch. Stanisław August's mania for theatricals led him to have a stage erected on the islet in the pond near the Palace-on-the-Water. On the bank opposite, an earth amphitheatre with a canvas roof was raised, but the king dreamed of a stone or brick structure where he could entertain large numbers of guests. This was designed by Kamsetzer in 1790, modeled on the theatre at Herculaneum, with a stage door derived from the Roman temples at Baalbek. Sixteen famous playwrights' statues by Le Brun decorated the amphitheatre's upper parapet. One thousand people could be accommodated to watch the ballets and panto-mimes, and afterward guests were frequently entertained in a new little pavilion by Kamsetzer called the Turkish House, which was dismantled in the nineteenth century.

Around the grounds the pace of activity was no less frenetic. Both main ponds were given artificially informal shore lines and more waterfalls, while many different species of trees were planted. Bridges and statues were also added to the park, including in 1788 an equestrian statue of King Jan Sobieski by Franciszek Pinck.

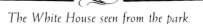

The White House seen from the park.

Copy of the tomb of Cecilia Metella in the park.

Jakub Kubicki's Egyptian Temple.

Stanisław August spent much of his time at Łazienki and seemed to be happiest there. He hosted an open-air festival with games in the park attended by around thirty thousand people; rowing on the canals also became one of his favorite occupations, and he had decorative steps constructed leading down to the water. Not all his plans were realized: the small mausoleum for his parents, in which he too wished to be buried, was never completed, nor was Kamsetzer's reconstruction of the baroque Belvedere Palace, or the vast church dedicated to Divine Providence, envisaged by Jakub Kubicki as a memorial to the constitution of 1791.

Retiring increasingly from the appalling problems confronting Poland, Stanisław August concentrated his energies on his private dream world at Łazienki. The court gathered there en masse in the summer, and the public was always admitted to the unfenced park if not the buildings. When forced to abdicate in 1795 he continued to send a flow of instructions concerning future improvements from his Russian exile until his death in 1798. The estate then passed to his heir and nephew, Józef Poniatowski. Four years after he perished at the Battle of Leipzig in 1813, Łazienki became the personal property of the Russian tsar. At his behest, Kubicki rebuilt the Belvedere Palace in a modest neoclassical style for the tsar's son Grand Duke Constantine in 1818; shortly afterward follies in the form of Diana and Egyptian temples were constructed, as well as a no-longer-extant neo-Gothic orangery, while the old Trou-Madame pavilion was transformed into a guardhouse. The grounds along the Vistula embankment were transformed into the estate's botanical gardens, and a large astronomical observatory developed by several architects replaced the king's extensive hothouses.

In 1846 an Orthodox church with a low dome in classical style was added to the west pavilion of the Palace-on-the-Water, although it was demolished a century later. Two new orangeries were also built to house the huge Radziwiłł collection of orange trees, brought from Nieborów.

The amphitheatre seen from across the lake.

Old view of the Palace-on-the-Water at night, by Zygmunt Vogel, late eighteenth century. (National Museum, Warsaw.)

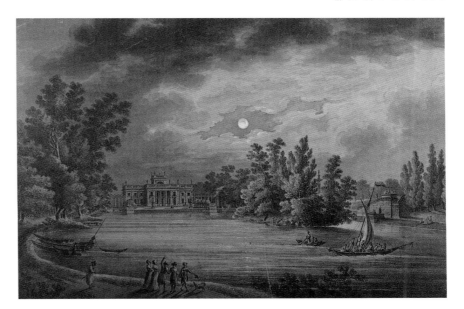

Although the palaces remained private, the park was maintained at a high standard as the city's principal public garden. As the trees matured, it was even expanded southward. Slight damage was caused in World War I, during which the contents of Łazienki were removed to Russia—although after independence they were returned safely. The new Polish government then removed the alterations done in tsarist times, and joined Łazienki's park with that of the Belvedere Palace (originally both parks had been one, but they had been divided in the nineteenth century). To symbolize its national importance, a monument to Fryderyk Chopin was erected there in 1926.

World War II brought far worse developments. Łazienki escaped the destruction that befell much of Warsaw in 1939, and the bulk of its contents were moved to the National Museum there for safekeeping. Under the German occupation, however, it was entirely closed to the public, and following the Warsaw Uprising in 1944, the rooms of the Palace-on-the-Water were burned when the Nazis poured petrol into them. Luckily German troops lacked the time to blow up the building too, as they had planned. Postwar reconstruction took twelve years, but at the end of that time the interiors of the Palace-on-the-Water, the White House, and the Old Orangery theatre had been painstakingly restored to their former glory, fitted with elegant furnishings both old and new and reopened to the public.

Today Łazienki, "Warsaw's Drawing Room" as it is sometimes nicknamed, stands again, a recreated model of eighteenth-century taste and a tribute to the vision and patronage of one man. With its lovely park, its rich variety of buildings, and the glorious Palace-on-the-Water, it would be hard to find a more delightful ensemble anywhere in the world. "A happy combination of Roman and French good taste," was how a visitor, the Abbé Renard, described the Old Orangery theatre in 1788, a remark that could be applied to the whole ensemble, with the coda, "and of Polish inspiration."

KOZŁÓWKA

The landscape of eastern Poland stretches, flat and unvarying, toward the frontier with the Soviet Union and its endless plains. Yet there are compensations—numerous beautiful monuments stand in the old city of Lublin and several fine chateaux and country houses can be found in the area. Of these, none is more charming or interesting than Kozłówka, situated some twenty miles or so north of Lublin near the little town of Lubartów.

The origins of the small settlement at Kozłówka are obscure, but soon after 1700 the property was recorded to have been owned by Jadwiga Niemyska, who also possessed several other estates. In 1728 she left everything to her niece Tekla Pepłowska, who brought a substantial dowry with her seven years later when she married Michał Bieliński, starosta or sheriff of Sztum. That same year Michał had ended a colorful marriage to Maria Rutowska, daughter of Augustus the Strong by his Turkish mistress, Fatima, thus enabling himself to take Tekla as his new bride some months later. The Bielińskis were a family who had risen high in the favor of the Saxon kings, one sister, Marianna, being one of Augustus the Strong's countless mistresses. Michał's elder brother, Franciszek, was marshal of the crown, an enlightened patron of the arts, and proprietor of the magnificent chateau of Otwock Stary. On Franciszek's death without issue in 1757, Michał's son, another Franciszek, succeeded to all the family estates.

By 1742 the Bielińskis had decided to build themselves a residence at Kozłówka. In fact by the mid-eighteenth century many aristocrats were busy constructing or improving houses in the vicinity: the Czartoryskis at Puławy, the Lubomirskis at Opole, the Potockis at Radzyń Podlaski, and the Sanguszkos at Lubartów. Kozłówka was originally intended as a *maison de plaisance* in the French sense, used for short stays by its owners—in contrast to the typical Polish country house, which was meant to be the center of a working estate. Architecturally, however, the country seat built by the Bielińskis was typical of the period, consisting of a single two-story block covered by a mansard roof and situated on an axis between the courtyard and the garden. The reception rooms and the private apartments of the owners were placed on the second floor, the ground level being occupied by administrative and domestic offices along with their two sons' rooms. At Kozłówka the ground floor was divided by a corridor which ran across the entire breadth of the house behind the large entrance hall; rooms opened off either side, not in a long enfilade as in grander buildings. In one corner upstairs a small chapel led off Tekla's bedroom.

In the front the large lawn was framed by stables and the kitchen block on one side with the coach house on the other, although the effect was slightly marred by the lack of anything to balance off the kitchen. On the other side an avenue ran straight from the house toward a fairly small park, laid out traditionally with a parterre in the Renaissance style adjoining the chateau and a flower and vegetable garden along its southern edge. There were no terraces, fountains, or statuary, for the grounds of

View of the fountain and the garden facade of Kozłówka, eastern Poland near Lublin.

the house were designed on the same modest scale as the interior.

Precise information about the architect employed by the Bielińskis is unfortunately lacking, but it can most probably be ascribed to Jakub Fontana. Originally Italian, his family had been settled in Poland since the mid-seventeenth century and his father, Józef, had worked mainly in and around Warsaw up to his death in 1741. At that point Jakub, aged about thirty and trained in Italy and Paris, took over his practice. The elder Fontana had already worked for the Bielińskis at Otwock Stary, and Kozłówka certainly has stylistic similarities to other buildings designed by the Fontanas. The family's less well known cousin Paweł Antoni Fontana may also have been involved, however; he had already been commissioned by the Sanguszkos for a new parish church at nearby Lubartów and continued to work in the Lublin region.

Born in 1740, the young Franciszek Bieliński inherited his uncle's and father's properties, married Krystyna Sanguszko, his neighbor, and led an active public life during Stanisław August's reign. As a politician with a close interest in education, he was appointed by the king to his commission for national education. Franciszek advocated universal schooling as well as the foundation of special craft schools where Polish rather than Latin would be the language of instruction. A fervent patriot, he joined Tadeusz Kościuszko's uprising and offered the whole of the produce from his estates to alleviate the people's suffering. By contrast his younger brother Stanisław was a rake and a drunkard with an evil reputation, a man willing to preside over the puppet Seym convened by Catherine the Great in 1793 to ratify the partitions of Poland. Thus family relations were inevitably strained. In 1799 Franciszek, despairing of both his family's and his country's future, sold Kozłówka and all its contents to Aleksander Zamoyski for 1.6 million zlotys.

Zamoyski was the head of the noble dynasty that had risen to prominence in the late sixteenth century with Jan, the builder of Zamość. The

Kozłówka seen through the entrance gates.

Stanisław Kostka Zamoyski with his wife, Zofia (née Czartoryska), and their family, by Józef Grassi, 1810.

View of the Red Salon, decorated with family portraits.

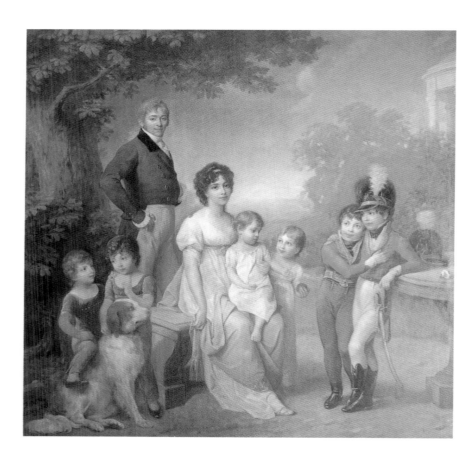

youthful son of Chancellor Andrzej Zamoyski, who had endeavoured to introduce many liberal reforms under Stanisław August, Aleksander had seemed destined for a distinguished career himself, but unfortunately he died suddenly in 1800. Since he was childless, Kozłówka was inherited by his sister Anna Sapieha, although his widow, Anna Maria, retained a life interest in the house. This she kept through two later marriages and a move to Vienna, where she died in 1846, bequeathing the contents of the chateau to her ward, Maria Soltan. Meanwhile ten years earlier Anna Sapieha had sold the property to her cousin Jan Zamoyski. This awkward situation resulted in an impasse and the house stood empty and unfurnished.

Jan, the new owner, was the son of Stanisław Kostka Zamoyski, who had succeeded his brother as head of the family and had managed to produce seven sons with his wife Zofia, daughter of the formidable chatelaine of Puławy, Izabella Czartoryska. Not surprisingly with such ancestry, two of Jan's six brothers became outstanding patriots: Andrzej, a noted agronomist and moderate politician, and Władysław, who went into exile in Paris in the wake of the rising of 1830, became the indispensable lieutenant of his uncle Adam Jerzy Czartoryski, and never ceased to work for Polish independence. Jan, however, was a very different character. Well-educated at Geneva and Berlin, where he had been a pupil of Friedrich

Hegel, he was possessed of a kind heart and a lively imagination. But he was by no means a practical man and found life a constant disillusionment. He did become an attaché at the Russian embassies in Naples and then in London, but resigned after the Polish revolt had been crushed in 1831. Fundamentally apolitical, Jan retired into private life and in 1843 married Anna Mycielska, a union blessed with two sons and a daughter. He only visited Kozłówka occasionally, bringing a few pieces of furniture and pictures from Puławy to enliven the empty house and adding others that his wife had inherited. Finally in the 1850s he closed the chateau and moved altogether to France, settling at Auteuil. During the rising of 1863 partisans sought refuge in Kozłówka, but luckily no damage was done.

A dramatic change in Kozłówka's fortunes occurred in 1870. According to land registry records, in September of that year Jan made over the estate to his son Konstanty. The latter had been born in Warsaw in 1846, but his formative years had been spent in France. His mother had died of tuberculosis when he was only thirteen, so his father had strictly supervised his education. In the late 1860s Konstanty had returned to Poland and trained in estate management, and in 1870 he had married Aniela Potocka shortly before settling into his new home. At last the chateau had a resident proprietor again, one who would live there until his death fifty-three years later.

There was indeed much to be done. No improvements and limited maintenance had taken place during the whole of the nineteenth century, so the buildings were in a dilapidated condition. The architect whom Konstanty consulted for all the changes he envisaged is unknown but was probably Leandro Marconi, one of the two sons of Enrico, the well-known exponent of late neoclassicism. It had definitely been Leandro whom he commissioned to build a city residence in Warsaw in 1878. The remodeling of Kozłówka began shortly after that, lasting throughout the 1880s and 1890s and intermittently up to 1914. The style was essentially French baroque with various Polish touches. All the elevations were re-faced and two cupola-crowned towers were added at either end of the facade. The side elevations also acquired pillared arcades, above which terraces were created on the second-floor level with balustrades adorned by groups of sculpted putti.

Mantel in the Red Salon with Boulle clock and four Meissen figures.

Portraits of the four young sons of Stanisław Kostka Zamoyski by Firmina Massot, 1819.

A monumental portico rising the entire height of the building was added to the front elevation, giving it a much heavier appearance. At ground level the portico was made into a vaulted covered porch behind an open arcade, approached from the drive by a raised ramp for carriages. The massive pediment bore a shield with the Zamoyski coat of arms, a device of three spears known as a *jelita*. (The legend ran that Florian the Grey, a Zamoyski ancestor, had received three spear wounds in the abdomen from the Teutonic Knights at the Battle of Płowce. Asked by the king if he was in great pain, he replied theatrically, "It hurts less than the wounds inflicted on the Fatherland.") A new entrance sealed the drive in the form of a wrought-iron gate surmounted by the family crest, which hung between two gate piers topped by stone urns. A row of domestic offices now flanked the drive on either side for most of its length.

Less evident were the changes made inside the chateau. The rear of the ground-floor hall was partitioned into three sections, the outer two of which were transformed into two more bathrooms. The walls of the grand staircase, which led off the middle space, were lined in white marble while a splendid wrought-iron stair-rail was brought from Warsaw. The second floor reception rooms were all redecorated in a neobaroque or neorococo taste that could more properly be described as eclectic, with rich stucco ornamentation, marble fireplaces in a variety of colors, and mahogany doors with gilt details. Fine parquet floors of light and dark oak made by local workmen were also installed. Despite the sumptuous decor,

Portrait of Anna Zamoyska (née Mycielska) by Claude-Marie Dubufy, mid-nineteenth century.

Portrait of Jan Zamoyski by Claude-Marie Dubufy, mid-nineteenth century.

however, the rooms seemed rather uniform as well as ostentatious in a fin-de-siècle way.

As a typical product of his class and era, Konstanty was keen to stress the cultural role of the aristocracy, so the collections he established at Kozłówka were intended to inculcate a sense of history and of patriotism in visitors. Eventually the number of pictures grew to almost one thousand altogether, many of them copies, family portraits, or canvases depicting scenes from Polish history, although there were a few Old Masters and a quantity of splendidly-carved frames. With a house so denuded of contents, the Zamoyskis brought in furniture from everywhere, often French but in the main nineteenth-century reproductions. A large library with some ten thousand volumes in English-style bookcases was created and elsewhere a big display of Chinese porcelain was installed. In 1904 Konstanty began to construct a chapel based on the upper half of the chapel at Versailles, with French altar ornaments and fine plasterwork; the tomb of his grandmother Zofia was also copied from one in the Church of Santa Croce at Florence, yet the effect is curiously cold. During the early years of the century the tsar consented to form an entail out of the Kozłówka estate, then extending to nearly fifty thousand acres, thus safeguarding it against being broken up in the future. The property suffered no significant damage in World War I, although a few shells did land on the roof. Konstanty died in 1923, by then a lonely widower, although his intellect and sense of humor had remained unimpaired and he had kept up a multitude of good works until the end. His first cousin, Adam Zamoyski, then succeeded him. Adam had led a busy public life both before and after Polish independence, having earlier lived in Saint Petersburg and having

Statuary group of putti on the roof.

View of the Billiard Room.

Members of the Zamoyski and Branicki families on the terrace at Kozłówka, c. 1910.

been appointed aide-de-camp to Tsar Nicholas II in 1916. In the revolution of 1917 he had been with the imperial family at Tsarskoë Seloe and had strongly advised them to flee to Finland. Despite his Russian connections he was nevertheless a good patriot, holding a string of civic offices in the 1920s and erecting in Kozłówka's park a memorial to the Polish dead from the campaign of 1812. Otherwise he made no changes to the appearance of the chateau.

Adam died in 1940 and his son Aleksander succeeded. But as a cavalry officer he was immediately arrested by the Germans and imprisoned in a concentration camp. His wife, Jadwiga, remained at Kozłówka, which became a sanctuary for their relatives and other refugees including the future Cardinal Stefan Wyszyński; arms for the resistance were also hidden in the chateau's cellars. Jadwiga moved to Warsaw in 1944, unfortunately taking many of the best contents with her, some of which were stored in the National Museum's depots. Everything was completely destroyed when the residents of the capital rose against the German occupation that summer. Kozłówka itself remained undamaged, and the new Communist regime took over the property and the surviving collection in November 1944. The Zamoyskis emigrated to Canada after their home was declared to be a museum, but its contents and fabric continued to decay for over twenty years. Finally a major restoration was belatedly undertaken, after which the chateau, once more in proper condition, reopened to the public in 1976.

Kozłówka is not the most famous of Poland's great houses, nor can it claim the interesting historical associations of many of its peers. Moreover its position far to the east, albeit just off the main road north from Lublin, makes it less easily accessible. Yet it stands as a splendid monument to Konstanty Zamoyski, a great collector of wide-ranging tastes and a member of one of Poland's most distinguished families. Kozłówka is likely to delight those who appreciate fine things, opulent decor, and the opportunity to see an aristocrat's chateau much as it must have looked in its glory days before World War I.

AFTERWORD

There are few virtues that the Poles do not possess—and there are few mistakes they have ever avoided." Winston Churchill's dictum is equally true today; Poland's history of heroism and defeat, of grandeur and pathos, is both unique and tragic. In the past sixteen years the Communist regime has collapsed, and Soviet troops have finally left the country. Poland is an enthusiastic member of NATO and more recently has joined the European Union. Its politics are genuinely democratic; both the Solidarity party and the reformed Communists have gained and lost power. Recently a right-wing government has replaced a long-serving president, formerly a Communist minister. Against this background, how have the nation's country houses fared, and, equally pertinent, what has been done to restore the rights of their erstwhile owners?

Arriving in Warsaw, any visitor is struck by the evident changes. The city is booming, real estate values are soaring, and there is a general sense of purpose, in marked contrast to the prevalent gloom of the late 1980s. Certainly drab, poor housing is still widespread, but the pace of restoration in the city center is impressive. The paralytic drunks once to be seen on almost every street corner have entirely vanished. Along with much new construction, many old buildings are being converted or refurbished. Even the gingerbread monstrosities of Stalinist architecture, which used to dominate the city center, now form an almost quaint feature of the landscape.

The Royal Castle well encapsulates this progress. Entirely rebuilt from its wartime ruins, it was a tribute to Polish patriotic determination and skillful restoration in the Communist era. Now it is all gleaming perfection—the decoration flawless, the contents upgraded. More rooms have been opened to the public, and work continues. There are now plans to restore the grounds, close the unsightly embankment road that cuts off the castle from the Vistula, and thus re-create the park as it must have looked at the time of Stanisław August.

Wilanów has always been Warsaw's answer to Versailles, although Jan Sobieski did not live there long enough to impose his personality on it as the Sun King did at his palace and the varied procession of owners in the two and a half centuries following his death ensured that Wilanów never became a monument to one era. The Communist regime brought in furniture and pictures from other houses, further destroying Wilanów's original identity. Fifteen years ago the buildings both inside and out were in fair shape, although some of the decor was looking a little tired.

The contrast offered by its present state is almost unbelievable. Though closed to the public for the winter, on my visit Wilanów presented a perfect hive of activity. Everywhere there were workmen, painters, gilders, and scaffolding. In most of the rooms the pictures had been taken off the walls, and the dust-sheeted furniture was crowded into the middle of the rooms to facilitate the thorough recleaning, rehanging, and partial redecoration. Some rooms, like the King's Apartments, were already finished and looked immaculate; others, like the Queen's Apartments, were in a state of chaos. Some objects moved to other houses have been tracked down and returned, while a few of quite different provenance have been removed, so that Wilanów's contents today may be nearly the same as when in the Branickis' hands—no mean feat, given the lack of prewar inventories. There are now over 6,000 artifacts in the palace, although a further 500 are still missing.

The energetic young director proudly explained he had many other plans for the palace as funds became available. The exterior was gradually

Old view of Wilanów, by Bernardo Bellotto, 1776, page 77

The White House, Łazienki, page 112

being repainted in a daring shade of vivid yellow, a dramatic contrast to the ubiquitous "Schönbrünn *gelb*" of Central Europe, while all the statuary and trophies were carefully picked out in white and terra-cotta, which research has shown were the original bright colors used. It will be interesting to see if other houses follow suit. A modern ventilation system is also to be installed, and the grounds, long neglected, are to be improved too; the seventeenth-century Italianate garden at the rear will eventually be restored to its original glory, replacing the ugly concrete paving. In 2007 a conference will be held at the palace to discuss the plans submitted by Brian Dixon, who re-created the seventeenth-century gardens at Hampton Court. Wilanów is certainly a triumph. Every year it has 115,000 foreign and Polish visitors, but numbers can only be dramatically improved with a modern ventilation system.

Łazienki, the capital's other palace complex, seemed in even more immaculate condition. The Palace-on-the-Water, although shut up for the winter months, was as elegant as ever, its superb neoclassical ballroom the perfect setting for Stanisław August's round of parties. The remnants of the king's picture collection still hang upstairs. Only in the White House were there signs of disruption; pictures, furniture, and objects were strewn around in a large program of rearrangement and redecoration, though the chinoiserie decor will remain unchanged.

Indeed, at Łazienki today the exteriors rather than the interiors are receiving the most attention. The original vistas are being re-created by cutting back overgrown trees and bushes. The waterworks, one of the main features of the park, are being overhauled and reconnected. Several of the smaller ornamental buildings, the reproduction of the Tomb of Cecilia Metella, and Jakub Kubicki's monumental Egyptian temple, where part of the roof has apparently collapsed, are being repaired. There are plans for more musical and theatrical performances during the summer. For years Łazienki, now entirely surrounded by Warsaw's urban sprawl, has been the city's drawing room; now it may be hoped that it will be fully brought back to life.

It would indeed be extraordinary if all Poland's country houses were maintained to the standards set at Wilanów and Łazienki. And of course they are not, as is soon evident at Nieborów. This chateau, some fifty miles west of Warsaw, adjoins Arkadia, the most famous romantic landscape park in the country, created by Helena Radziwiłł in the late eighteenth century. Both are in a fair state of repair, but in both cases an imaginative touch would do wonders to enhance their charms.

Nieborów did retain pictures and some furniture of high quality, and this is still the case. The interiors are pleasant and elegant, without being spectacular, and have changed little in the past fifteen years. The feeling of intimacy suited to what was once a family home is lacking, as is any impression that Nieborów belonged to one of Poland's greatest dynasties. Limited redecoration has been undertaken in a few rooms, with rather mixed results, as most of the fabrics and wall coverings used are of poor quality. The problem, as the director soon confided, is essentially financial. For the past decade almost all country houses have had to supplement their grant from central funds by raising a proportion of their income locally. Nieborów, not uniquely, resorts to hosting paying guests in the outbuildings, banquets in the house, and the occasional wedding. In fact, those prepared to pay the price have been allowed to stay in the main apartments. Managing Nieborów like an amateur part-time hotel is not the answer to its problems.

The chateau may need a fairy godfather, but the extraordinary landscape garden adjoining the park requires one yet more urgently. Repairs at Arkadia have been undertaken when necessary; they have just been completed at the Temple of Diana, although no attempt was made to use the capacious interior for an exhibition to illustrate the history and symbolic importance of the place. Indeed, there is not one label visible in the whole of Arkadia. Other lesser follies—the Hermitage and High Priest's Sanctuary, for example—do need attention, and some of the bricks across one tier of the Aqueduct have been raised but not relaid.

Temple of Sibyl, Puławy, page 101

However, it is the landscape itself that makes the park a gloomy place. The original plans boasted several sheets of water, culminating in the Big Pond and the so-called River of Forgetfulness, where the traveler could forget his cares and worries. Today their levels are low, while other sizable excavations of uncertain origin also contain some water, as if by accident. No new planting appears to have been done, although a few trees have already been lost. Worst of all, a hideous conifer is being nurtured on a hillock, a tree unknown to a picturesque landscape. On a winter afternoon, Arkadia presented a forlorn spectacle to its only visitors, at once unkempt and unloved.

If Nieborów and Arkadia evoke memories of an idyllic past, Puławy's appeal is more poignant still—while one represents the spirit of aristocratic escapism, the other glorifies the ideal of patriotic sacrifice. The Czartoryski family created one of Poland's foremost artistic monuments at Puławy, only to have it twice confiscated from them by the Russians. The family's direct connection here ended over 175 years ago, but its spirit lives on today.

The big house, once so imposing, is a gaunt, lifeless shell. In military or institutional use since the 1830s, it serves today as the headquarters of an agrarian institute-cum-museum. None of the interiors survive, nor do any original contents. The rooms are painted in tones of uniform ugliness, while some of the grander spaces have been crudely partitioned for administrative convenience. Seldom should it be said that a house is beyond redemption; yet even given limitless time and money, Puławy is probably a lost cause.

The important buildings in the park are not yet lost, however. Izabella Czartoryska's monument to Polish history and Chrystian Piotr Aigner's Temple of the Sibyl are in reasonable repair, although the stonework needs attention. The Polish historical monument's peerless position, on a bluff overlooking the valley of the Vistula, miraculously remains unchanged, although the surrounding park is shabby and poorly maintained. The Greek house, of slightly later date, has also kept its charm and has been well restored, while the museum contained in its six tiny rooms has been painstakingly displayed. The Gothic folly is also in reasonable shape, but no more. Given the number of rich Polish expatriates, especially in the United States, is it too much to hope one could become the fairy godfather or godmother for the park at Puławy?

Traveling on through eastern Poland, a visit to Lublin provides reassuring evidence that much of the country has made steady progress during the past fifteen years. A whiff of old Osteuropa may still be detected in such a remote provincial town, but its shops and streets bespeak modest prosperity. The castle, with its wonderful chapel and the picturesque old town, seems well cared for, while among the chateaus in the surrounding countryside, none is in better condition than Kozłówka.

The former property of the Bielińskis, then the Zamoyskis, lies in a somewhat featureless landscape north of Lublin. As soon as the visitor turns through the gates, however, it becomes obvious that a high standard of maintenance has been kept. The grounds, for there was never a real garden here, are immaculately kept, the lawns of as high a quality as anywhere in Poland. The exterior of the chateau, essentially in French neo-Baroque taste, looked impeccable and had clearly enjoyed several coats of fresh paint recently.

Kozłówka has had varying fortunes in its history; substantially rebuilt over the end of the nineteenth century, it was abandoned after World War II and only properly restored again during the 1970s. It was therefore already in a good state when seen in the late 1980s, and is in still better shape today. Fortunately most of its contents, apart from those destroyed in Warsaw in 1944, have survived intact. The fine library, the billiard room, and the collection of Chinese porcelain all live up to a standard found in few other Polish houses. A degree of rearrangement and redecoration has

Entrance gates, Kosłowka, page 118

been undertaken, mostly very well, while the curatorial staff clearly takes great pride in their property. It is no wonder that more than 250,000 visitors come to visit every year.

Indeed, their long-standing director, en poste for over twenty years, was nearly responsible recently for a deal unique in Poland. After building good relations with the Zamoyski family, still living in Canada, he sponsored an agreement whereby for a fixed sum of several million dollars, payable from the public purse, the Zamoyskis renounced their rights to the property and contents of Kozłówka, thus recognizing the expropriation of 1945. It was a not ungenerous deal. Unfortunately a family adviser told them to sue for more, so matters remain at an impasse.

At present the most heartening example of private ownership and initiative is provided not by any individual house or property in Poland, but by a small model Renaissance town, created by the whim of a clever magnate over five centuries ago. Zamołł lies in modern Poland's southeast corner, and its very geographical remoteness makes the place all the more remarkable. The visitor is nearer to the Ukrainian frontier than to Lublin, the closest major city.

Fifteen years ago, under a light coating of snow, Zamołł clearly possessed considerable charm. The properties of the main square, the pretty houses along the side streets, the geographically proportioned layout were all there. But the painted facades were often drab or shabby, various architectural features needed repairs, and, with few shops or cafés, the town lacked life. Fortunately there had been little war damage or tasteless development, yet the spark to revitalize Zamołł was obviously lacking.

What a difference the intervening period and one remarkable man have made! Marcin Zamoyski has always lived in the locality, and following the fall of communism he was appointed *voivode*, or governor, of the surrounding region. Since then he has served two terms as the town's mayor, and it is his dedication and vision, aided by a number of willing collaborators, that have remade Zamołł. The center has been closed to wheeled traffic, and almost all the buildings have been restored and painted various cheerful shades of their original vivid colors. Many shops have opened, the quality and variety of which would be improved by more visitors, while there are plenty of cafés and restaurants, although the number of hotel beds has to date been limited.

An excellent museum opened, occupying two of the extravagantly gabled merchant houses almost adjoining the town hall and providing much historical information on the town and the Zamoyski family, with exhibits skillfully displayed. A splendidly robust equestrian statue of the founder, Jan Zamoyski, was specially commissioned by the council and recently erected in front of his former palace. This large building occupies much of one side of the central zone. Further embellished in the eighteenth century, it was severely damaged by the nineteenth-century Russian occupation. Now there are plans to complete Zamołł's restoration and provide a much-needed hotel. Everywhere are signs of urban revival, of new enterprise, of an enthusiasm for the future. The essentially apolitical mayor, an impressive yet modest figure, is rightly revered by the townspeople. One of his dedicated staff believes that Zamołł's potential is enormous, and that only the lack of any airport in the vicinity precludes a decent number of tourists. The hope must be that this can be achieved, so long as development of the modest suburbs and of hotel accommodation remains tightly controlled and the town center, one of Poland's jewels, stays as beautifully preserved.

The next house on the itinerary, Baranów, returns the traveler to earth with a bump: if Zamołł radiates brightness, warmth, and confidence in the future, Baranów offers nothing of the kind. Approached from the north or east through a polluted subindustrial zone, shut in from the nearby Vistula by high embankments, the castle could hardly have a more unpromising environment. Its entrance is unexpected too, partway along a hedge of bedraggled conifers lining the road, with modern apartment blocks interspersed along it. Worse yet, the eye is drawn to the left, where a hideous modern hotel, built in the 1990s, occupies one corner of the compound. The whole complex has been under the dead hand of the misnamed Agency for the Development of Industry.

It is easy to forget that Baranów was one of the finest Renaissance buildings in the country, but the paintwork on the external walls is in reasonable condition, and the courtyard is as splendid as ever. The elegant black-and-gold carved iron front door with the sundial perched above it is still imposing. The vaulted double staircase, with its ceiling covered with heraldic devices; the two tiers of arcades, with their elegant columns; and the row of huge grotesque heads (or mascaroons) all substantiate the castle's claim to architectural distinction.

This cannot be said of Baranów's interiors, which are an unmitigated disaster. The lack of virtually any decent pictures or furniture, plus the haphazard arrangement of the contents, bears witness to the fact that Baranów was for years run by a chemical company rather than by the national museum service. Tylman van Gameren's long picture gallery, a potentially stunning room, still displays a row of insipid nineteenth-century Italian landscapes, described volubly by a guide to a dejected-looking coach tour. This was the moment of the entire trip most redolent of old Osteuropa and its low standards. Beautiful is a word that may still be used to describe Baranów's proportions and architecture, but it can no longer be called satisfying by any modern criteria regulating the opening of a country house museum.

Yet again, the pendulum swung sharply back to the positive on my arrival at

Baranów, page 69

Łańcut. Arguably the grandest country house in Poland, it is not to everyone's taste: it has been criticized as "heavy," "overpowering," and "unimaginative." Nevertheless there is plenty for the visitor to see, even if most of the contents have been imported from other properties, since Alfred Potocki removed the cream of the collection before the end of World War II. And the number of improvements made over the last fifteen years is very encouraging.

In one virtually disused corner of the chateau a small hotel was created, for which there had been a crying need, as there was no bearable accommodation for many miles in any direction. Attached to it is a reasonable restaurant, a very necessary stop for the weary traveler before embarking on what is quite a marathon tour of the house and grounds. Indeed for any lover of Polish history, or of monumental interiors, there is probably enough of interest at Łańcut for a two-day visit.

The major rooms—the Ballroom, the Viennese Room, the Sculpture Gallery, the Hall of Columns—are as impressive as ever. Meanwhile some of the smaller reception rooms and bedchambers have been redecorated, and their contents—especially the pictures, the field in which postwar Łańcut was weakest—upgraded. For the first time the extensive library, occupying a hitherto unopened part of the chateau, is on show. The crammed bookshelves contain some volumes of antiquarian interest as well as a collection of reading books in several languages, such as a rich and cosmopolitan aristocratic family might have amassed in the nineteenth and early twentieth centuries. Indeed it has remained fossilized since the interwar period, with glossy magazines from the 1920s.

Outside, the building is immaculately well kept, as are the grounds. The manège, or riding school, with its striking frieze of horse heads, is open, as are the carriage house and stables just across the street, with their enormous

Court theater, Łańcut, page 59

collection of motorcars and coaches. A new carriage museum opened in a building to the rear, dedicated to the horse, with a huge harnessing hall in the middle and the so-called Black and Yellow carriage houses on either side, containing between them some fifty coaches of all kinds. There are also many hunting trophies, racing pictures, and some interesting equestrian statuary. Yet for all its grandeur, Łańcut lacks life and warmth; gradually the family is returning to use the house for weddings and other parties, and hopefully this is a development that can be much encouraged.

No greater contrast in style can be provided than by the last house on the itinerary. The castle of Pieskowa Skała lies only a few miles north of Kraków in the narrow, wooded Ojców Valley. The property had lacked a proper family of owners for some time, so it was in poor condition by the end of World War II. Indeed the very fabric of the castle, perched on a dramatic rock, was in some danger of collapse until the State Monuments Commission began a thoroughgoing restoration, both outside and inside the house, in 1950.

The dramatic situation of Pieskowa Skała's massive walls, the rectangular Renaissance courtyard with its two-story arcaded galleries and rich sculptural decoration, all mark the castle as one of the major medieval and sixteenth-century monuments of Poland. Fortunately there is much more to see inside the building than the splendid fortifications imply. The castle has had the good fortune to be attached to the Wawel in Kraków, one of the major European museums, and has benefited accordingly.

A variety of exhibits, ranging from earliest times to the end of the seventeenth century, was already in place through twelve rooms on the second floor fifteen years ago. Now a further six rooms have been opened on the third floor, all in galleries well arranged and lit, which continue the exhibits on through the next three hundred years to the modern age. The exhibits are not all of first-rate quality, but there are a number of fine or interesting objects on show, while the exhibition succeeds in its task of guiding the visitor through eight or nine centuries of history into the modern era. Pieskowa Skała can only ever be an imposing medieval castle whose heyday was long ago, but it is a splendid relic of the distant past.

Distance is the great enemy in Poland, and on a trip necessarily circumscribed by time and by the approach of winter, many of the houses described in the original volume remained unvisited. The whole of the western part of the country was omitted, although in fact this involved not visiting only one of the houses first described in a chapter of its own— Gołuchów, which is apparently in good shape, but substantially unchanged from fifteen years ago. Of the remainder previously seen: Nowy Wiłnicz, Radzył Podlaski, Otwock Stary, Walewice, Mała Wieł, Rogalin, Pawłowice, Smiełów, Jabłonna, Natolin, Kórnik, Klemensov, and Krasiczyn (to name but a few), one or two are, I believe, still virtual ruins, but most have been entirely or partly restored. And of this number most, given enough time and energy, well merit a visit from the discerning traveler.

Considering their limited finances and the many other calls on the national treasury, the Poles have looked after most of their more important country houses reasonably well, although, sadly, what remains of the *dvori*, or small manor houses of the petty gentry (of which three thousand were said to exist pre-1939, while now only a few survive), are usually left to crumble away to dust. Restoration at the level of Wilanów or Łazienki is of a superlatively high standard, one of the scant benefits of Soviet communism, which liberally promoted it from the 1950s. And in other cases the very remoteness of some country houses, where the local authorities are poor and timid, has saved them from tasteless redecoration or ostentatious overgilding.

The central paradox for most outsiders is, Why there has been little or no restitution of property to its former prewar owners? In the early 1990s, after the Iron Curtain had finally collapsed, hopes were as high in Poland as anywhere in Eastern Europe that justice would at last be done. After all, so many noble families opted to stay, sometimes in pretty wretched conditions, rather than choose the siren call of exile. In Hungary those members of the upper classes who had not already fled west in 1945 did so almost to a man after the failure of the 1956 uprising. In the former Czechoslovakia a surprisingly large number did remain after 1945, despite all the horrors, yet virtually every surviving aristocrat left after the crushing of the Prague Spring in 1968.

Not so in Poland. Despite the riots and repression, the show trials and the religious persecution, the nobility and gentry stayed behind in large numbers. The incentive to do so was hardly higher than elsewhere, with discrimination against the aristocracy a definite reality. Yet the obstinate patriotism that had enabled so many to adapt or survive nearly a century and a half of foreign occupation lingered undaunted. The government, nervous of making martyrs, tended to ignore people if they kept a low profile. Thus it was that some representative of almost every great Polish name could always be tracked down somewhere within the country.

But no national government, of any political persuasion, has shown the slightest inclination to tackle the problem. Thus, almost unbelievably, the 1945 Reform Act, which confiscated all holdings of more than fifty acres of private land, remains on the statute book today. Admittedly, in the past decade the courts have become slightly more liberal in interpreting the law; for example, if a house and garden can be shown to be quite separate from any business, the government is prepared to agree that it could be regarded as private property. The fact that any major estate depends, as it has always done, on a multiplicity of enterprises to survive proves the artificiality of the argument.

Courtyard arcades, Pieskowa Skała, page 51

Land reform itself has always been regarded as too hot a potato for any government to tackle. The problem in Poland lies in the fact that the landowners' confiscated estates were not, as in former Czechoslovakia or Hungary, turned into collective farms, but were often distributed piecemeal among the peasants. So today Poland has the largest number of individual farmers and one of the biggest agricultural sectors of any country in the European Union. The private part of the agrarian economy has consistently proved more productive than its state counterpart, indeed frequently helping to bail the state out in time of food shortages.

Houses and their contents provide a less contentious issue. In some cases, as at Łańcut, an enlightened director has encouraged family involvement with their old homes. Potockis have been welcomed back, even allowed to hold a family wedding and stay in their house. Rogalin, near Poznał, once the Raczynski chateau, has been turned into a foundation; family members sit on the board, occupy flats, and have a say in the running of the house.

Krasiczyn, the great Renaissance castle in far southeastern Poland, well illustrates these problems. Like all country houses it was expropriated in 1945, and only since the demise of communism has the government had any communication with the Sapiehas, the former owners. Unfortunately the castle is in the charge of the Agency for the Development of Industry, the very same Orwellian body that runs Baranów. When Michael Sapieha, a Belgian resident, pointed out how little the agency had actually done and instigated a lawsuit to recover his property, the agency suddenly began extensive restoration that he could never hope to repay. Conferences are now frequently held there in the new hotel built in the stables. The family may visit but have no say as to whether the huge interiors, ruinous and devoid of contents, should be restored.

As a generalization, private property in Poland has been most successfully recovered through the courts, though this is often a lengthy process. The Europaiski Hotel in the capital has just recently been given back to its former owners after a fifteen-year lawsuit. On the whole it has proved a little easier to succeed with restitution claims in the Kraków, rather than the Warsaw, area. The Czartoryski Museum, one of the most charming private collections in existence, was rapidly returned to its foundation board by the state; indeed it was then discovered that the museum had never really been nationalized at all, yet in the postwar chaos no one had actually noticed.

Most aristocratic families nowadays lack the money to move back into their ancestral homes, even if such an offer were made. If the land and enterprises that have traditionally supported the costs of the house are excluded from the deal, a substantial income from other sources, or generous subvention by the state, is essential. Today another important supply of additional revenue is excluded: the profits from the rich lands in the east with two or more crops per year were important even to a property like Łańcut, and, alas, are seemingly forever lost to the Ukraine or Belarus.

The Polish state has in the past promised to compensate landowners for property thus lost in the east, but to date it has never done so. The predictable result is an impasse, whereby the issue is quietly shelved as too expensive and complicated to tackle. The maze of conflicting Polish and German claims and counterclaims has been annulled by mutual agreement. Thus the likelihood of the former owners of landed property within the state's modern boundaries receiving any compensation at all, let alone one remotely realistic, is nil.

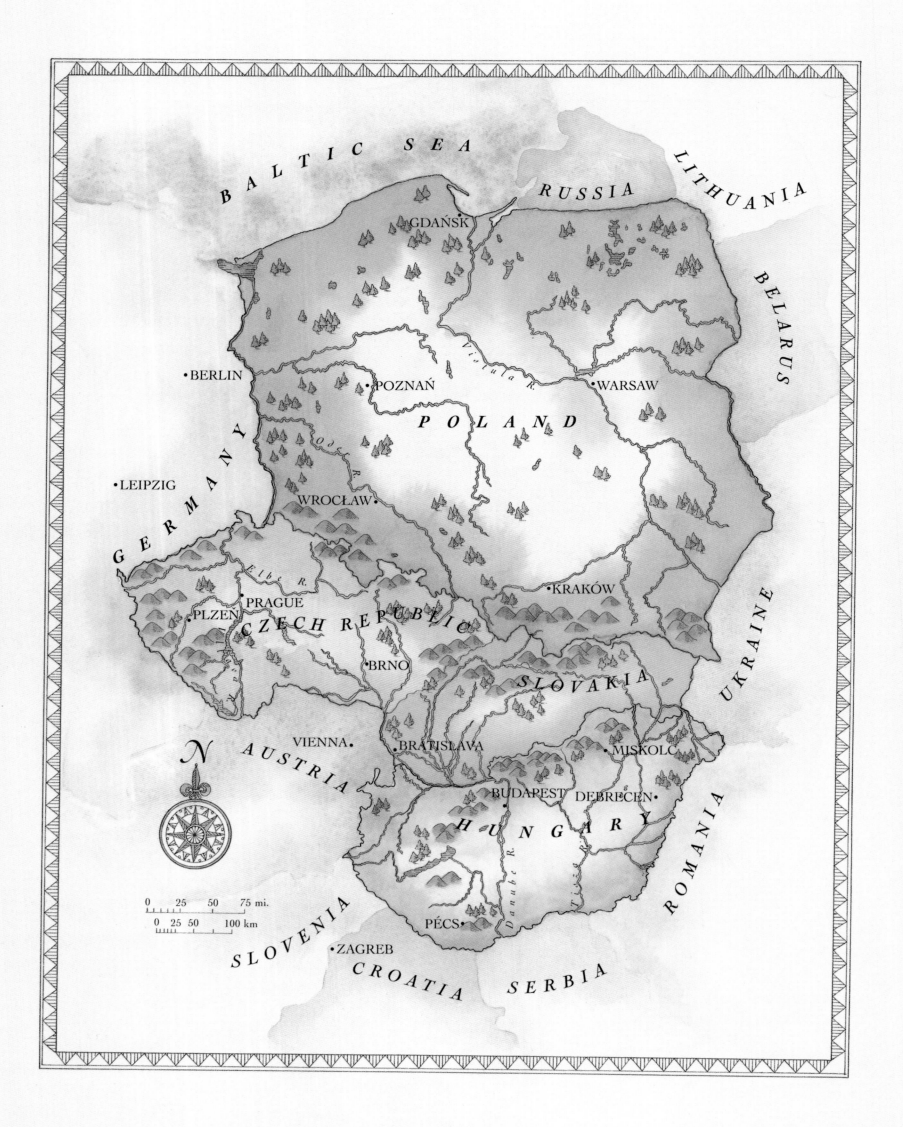

SELECTED BIBLIOGRAPHY

Branicka Wolska, Anna. *Unposted Letters.* Warsaw, 1990.

Coxe, William. *Travels in Poland.* London, 1792.

De Ligne, Prince Antoine. *Memoirs.* London, 1899.

Evans, R.J.W. *The Making of the Habsburg Monarchy, 1550–1700.* London, 1979.

Fabre, J. *Stanislas Auguste Poniatowski et L'Europe des Lumieres.* Paris, 1952.

Fijałkowski, Wojciech. *The Residence-Museum at Wilanów.* Warsaw, 1986.

Gieysztor, A., and A. Rottermund. *The Royal Castle in Warsaw.* Warsaw, 1982.

Jabłoński, K., and W. Piwkowski. *Nieborów and Arkadia.* Warsaw, 1988.

Knox, Brian. *The Architecture of Poland.* London, 1971.

Konarski, G. *La Noblesse Polonais.* Paris, 1958.

Kozakiewicz, H. and S. *The Renaissance in Poland.* Warsaw, 1976.

Lednicki, Wacław. *The Life and Culture of Poland.* New York, 1944.

Majewska-Maszkowska, B. *The Château of Łańcut.* Warsaw, 1964.

Morton, V. B. *Sobieski, King of Poland.* Glasgow, 1944.

Ostrawska-Kebłowska, Zofia. *Palace Architecture in Greater Poland in the Later Eighteenth Century.* Poznań, Poland, 1969.

Perey, Lucien. *Histoire d'une grande dame.* Paris, 1888.

Potocki, Count Alfred. *Master of Łańcut.* London, 1959.

Radziwiłł, Prince Michael. *One of the Radziwiłłs.* London, 1971.

Reddaway, W. J. *The Cambridge History of Poland.* 2 vols. Cambridge, England, 1951.

Siegert, Hans, and F. Peer. *Das Bleibt vom alten Osterreich.* Vienna, 1978.

Sitwell, Sacheverell. *Great Houses of Europe.* London, 1961.

Sołtyński, Roman. *Glimpses of Polish Architecture.* Warsaw, 1958.

Zamoyski, Count Adam. *The Polish Way.* London, 1987.

Żygulski, Zdzisław. *The Czartoryski Collection,* Warsaw, 1978.

Library, Nieborów, page 90

PRONUNCIATION GUIDE

Arkadia (ar-KAH-dyah)
Baranów (bah-RAH-nooff)
Gołuchów (go-WOO-hooff)
Kozłówka (kuzz-WOOFF-kah)
Łańcut (WAHN-tsoot)
Łazienki (wah-JYEN-kee)
Nieborów (neh-BOH-rooff)
Pieskowa Skała (PYESS-koh-vah SCOW-ah)
Puławy (poo-WAH-vih)
Wilanow (vee-LAH-nooff)

Staircase, Baranów, page 70

PRACTICAL GUIDE TO VISITING
THE GREAT COUNTRY HOUSES OF POLAND

Baranów

pages 67–73

Location: southern Poland on the Vistula River

CONTACT INFORMATION:

Museum - Zamek w Baranowie Sandomierskim
ul. Zamkowa 20, 39-450 Baranów
Sandomierski
Tel.: +48 (15) 811 80 40; 811 80 39; 811 85 04
Fax: +48 (15) 811 80 63

VISITING HOURS:

Year-round: 9:00 a.m. to 5:00 p.m., Sunday
and holidays; 9:00 a.m. to 2:30 p.m., Tuesday
through Saturday; closed Monday

HIGHLIGHTS:

Little Wawel courtyard

Gołuchów

pages 97–105

Location: west-central Poland

CONTACT INFORMATION:

Muzeum – Zamek w Gołochowie
Oddział Muzeum Narodowego w Poznaniu
63-322 Gołuchów
Tel./Fax: +48 (62) 761 50 94

VISITING HOURS:

Year-round: 10:00 a.m. to 4:00 p.m., closed
Monday
May 1 to September 30: also open 10:00 a.m.
to 5:00 p.m. on Sunday

HIGHLIGHTS:

Ancient Vases, Ancient, Gothic, Old Polish
Portrait, and Royal Rooms, along with a
neo-Renaissance chapel, the Czartoryski
Mausoleum, and the Forestry Museum

Neo-Rennaissance chapel, Gołuchow

Kozłówka

pages 117–125

Location: southeastern Poland

CONTACT INFORMATION:

Muzeum Zamoyskich w Kozłówce
21-132 Kamionka
Tel.: +48 (81) 852 80 00
Reservations: +48 (81) 852 83 10
Fax: +48 (81) 852 83 50

VISITING HOURS:

March 1 to November 30: 10:00 a.m. to 4:00
p.m., Tuesday through Friday; 10:00 a.m. to
4:00 p.m., Saturday through Sunday; closed
Monday and holidays
December 2 to December 15: 10:00 a.m. to
3:00 p.m., Tuesday through Sunday; closed
Monday and holidays

HIGHLIGHTS:

Palace building, chapel modeled after
Versailles, Theater, Guardhouse, Coach
House and Stable

Łańcut

pages 54–65

Location: southeastern Poland

CONTACT INFORMATION:

Zamek w Łałcucie
ul. Zamkowa 1, 37-100 Łańcut
Tel.: +48 (17) 225 20 08-10
Fax: +48 (17) 225 20 12

VISITING HOURS:

February to April and October to November:
10:00 a.m. to 2:00 p.m.
May to September: 9:00 a.m. to 2:30 p.m.,
Tuesday through Saturday; 9:00 a.m. to
2:00 p.m. Sunday
Closed Mondays, holidays, and during music
festival in May

HIGHLIGHTS:

The Coach House, Turkish and Chinese
Rooms, Red Corridor, Drawing Room, Dining
Room, Ball Room, and Private and Guest
Suites, Collection of Historic Clocks and
Musical Instruments

Billiard room, Kozłowka

Łazienki

pages 106–115
Location: Warsaw
CONTACT INFORMATION:
Łazienki Królewskie Museum
ul. Agrykoli 1
Tel.: +44 (22) 6218212
VISITING HOURS:
n/a
HIGHLIGHTS:
Palace and Theater on the Island, The White House, Hunting Palace, Hermitage, Old Orangery, Old Guardhouse, The Water Tower, Hall of Prominent Personalities, and Hall of Medallions

Nieborów and Arkadia

pages 84–95
Location: central Poland, near Łódź
CONTACT INFORMATION:
Muzeum w Nieborowie i Arkadii
Oddział Muzeum Narodowego w Warszawie
99-416 Nieborów
Tel./Fax: +48 (46) 838 56 35
website: www.nieborow.art.pl
VISITING HOURS:
May to September: 10:00 a.m. to 5:30 p.m., closed Monday
October to April: 10:00 a.m. to 4:00 p.m., closed Monday
Park open from 10:00 a.m. to dusk
HIGHLIGHTS:
Original interiors of eighteenth and nineteenth-century rooms, Radziwiłł Family library; Arkadia park with fanciful buildings: Murgrabia House, the Little Gothic House, Diana's Temple, Cave of Sibyl, Tomb of Illusions, and others

Pieskowa Skała

pages 46–53
Location: 30 km from Kraków
CONTACT INFORMATION:
Pieskowa Skała Castle Museum
32-045 Sułoszowa, woj. Małopolskie
Tel./Fax: +48 (12) 389 60 04
VISITING HOURS:
October to April: 10:00 a.m. to 3:30 p.m., closed Monday
May to September: 9:00 a.m. to 4:00 p.m., Tuesday through Thursday; 9:00 a.m. to 1:00 p.m., Friday; 10:00 a.m. to 6:00 p.m., Saturday, Sunday, and holidays; closed Monday
HIGHLIGHTS:
The two-storey sixteenth-century loggia, seventeenth-century chapel, late Gothic artillery tower, seventeenth-century ramparts, and mannerist gargoyles. On permanent display is an exhibition called *Changing Styles in European Art from the Middle Ages to the Early Eighteenth Century*

Wilanów

pages 75–83
Location: Warsaw
CONTACT INFORMATION:
Muzeum Pałac w Wilanowie
ul. Stanisława K. Potockiego 10/16
02-958 Warszawa
Tel.: +48 (22) 842 81 01 or 842 48 09
Reservations: +48 (22) 842 07 95
e-mail: muzeum@wilanow-palac.art.pl
VISITING HOURS:
Year-round 9:00 a.m. to 4:00 p.m., closed Tuesday, New Year's Day, Easter weekend, Corpus Christi, November 11, and Christmas Eve and Day
May 15 to September 18: also open 9:00 a.m. to 6:00 p.m., Wednesday; 9:00 a.m. to 7:00 p.m., Sunday
Park is open daily until dusk (free on Thursday)
HIGHLIGHTS:
Seventeenth, eighteenth, and nineteenth-century interiors, Polish Portrait Gallery, Chinese Rooms, Royal Suites of August II, Duchess Izabela Lubomirska's Suite, Wilanów Collections.

Amphitheater, Łazienki

Queen's bedroom interior, Wilanów

INDEX

Page numbers in *italics* refer to illustrations

INDEX